**Doing
Nothing**

Practices

A series edited by Margret Grebowicz

Doing Nothing by James Currie

Fly-Fishing by Christopher Schaberg

Juggling by Stewart Lawrence Sinclair

Raving by McKenzie Wark

Riding by Pardis Mahdavi

Running by Lindsey A. Freeman

Star Charting by Bess Matassa

Taking Leave by Deborah Kapchan

Tomorrowing by Terry Bisson

Doing Nothing

James Currie

DUKE UNIVERSITY PRESS
Durham and London
2026

Project Editor: Liz Smith
Designed by A. Mattson Gallagher
Typeset in Untitled Serif and General Sans
by Copperline Book Services

Library of Congress Cataloging-in-Publication Data
Names: Currie, James R., author.
Title: Doing nothing / James Currie.
Other titles: Practices.
Description: Durham : Duke University Press, 2026. | Series:
Practices | Includes bibliographical references.
Identifiers: LCCN 2025026140 (print)
LCCN 2025026141 (ebook)
ISBN 9781478033059 (paperback)
ISBN 9781478029601 (hardcover)
ISBN 9781478061816 (ebook)
Subjects: LCSH: Currie, James R. | Catastrophical, The. |
Catastrophical, The, in literature. | Mental illness. | Nothing
(Philosophy) | Civilization, Modern.
Classification: LCC BD375 .C87 2026 (print) | LCC BD375 (ebook)
LC record available at https://lccn.loc.gov/2025026140
LC ebook record available at https://lccn.loc.gov/2025026141

Cover text handwritten by James Currie.

In loving memory:

Lester McLennan (2004–2024)

Not for nothing

CONTENTS

Preface   ix
Acknowledgments   xxiii

Part 1. **About Me**   1

Part 2. **Cosmos**   37

Notes   75
Bibliography   77

Faced with the increasingly unlivable conditions of our times, where "too much" has become the presiding modality—where we work too much, expect too much of ourselves, are bombarded with too much information, overwhelmed by too much stimulation, and endlessly confronted with political and ecological catastrophes that are close to being too much for us to be able to do anything about, and sometimes too much even to conceptualize —many have started taking counsel from the idea that less is best, and that the injunction always to be "doing something" is as much a symptom of the disease from which we are suffering as it is a rallying cry for the making of a better world. As a result, slow movements proliferate in every sphere; wellness as opposed to success at any cost has become a discursive norm; a whole array of practices are now being sought out so that we might at last escape from the iron cage of the Protestant work ethic and live better; and an army of publications, blogs, and podcasts has marched onto our bookshelves and smartphone scrolls to school, inspire, and elucidate us regarding how this quiet revolution is to be achieved.

It would seem, then, to be a propitious historical moment in which to be writing about doing nothing. And indeed, in recent years, doing nothing has become increasingly viewed as admirable, useful, good, healthy, responsible, wholesome, ethical, civic-minded, effective, and evidence that you are not wasting your life. Doing nothing "is about being free to live the lives we want to lead, free from bosses, wages, commuting, consuming and debt." It is a "revolution brewing"—indeed, "the most enjoyable revolution the world has ever seen."[1] It can help working women and mothers achieve more by doing less.[2] When it appears as aimlessness, it has value and utility: It is "purposeful," the "directed randomness of nomadic life," an encyclopedic impulse where "paths are endless" and "possibility reigns"; it is a "fluid, fluctuating, unstable collection of expectations," an "aspiration," a "place where one takes time out in order to regroup and resurface in a new mode," an "intentional unintentionality," and "exactly what it takes to get some of us in motion, get us to bump into what we need to bump into."[3] To practice it is to join the path that leads to happiness.[4] As the blurb on the back of one book states, it is both "easily achievable" and "absolutely essential to leading an enjoyable and creative life."[5] And so it is the perfect antidote to a world where stress and burnout are on the rise.[6]

But doing nothing, as a result, has evidently now become the new means of doing something instead. It's depressing. Some of its present practitioners even call themselves out happily in this regard. One well-known author states that her book on the topic is a "field guide" that functions as "an act of political resistance" and "also a plan of action"; in the process of writing her book, she claims, she "inadvertently radicalized [herself] by learning the importance of *doing something*."[7] So what about doing nothing does this new ideology of doing nothing seek to avoid? Those aspects of our lives about which nothing can be done. This is what doing nothing has been for me: It is what I did when there was nothing that could be done.

My practice thus recuperates something of the proclivities of an unreconstructed doing nothing — of its unacceptability, brutal humor, fury, despair, poor behavior, and grand refusal of the inanity of team-player life. Unsavory at times, it is a challenge to the digestive system and might make you sick. Like the chthonic sovereign of some archaic realm, it is accompanied by a ghoulish retinue including procrastination, lassitude, torpor, apathy, immaturity, indifference, fatalism, resignation, bathos, exhaustion, indecisiveness, nihilism, inactivity, intransigence, failure, melancholia, introversion, and sleep. It is a hard sell. But if I assume it's too expensive, I will never make it out of the present deadlock. I'll remain stuck between forms of doing nothing that suffer from either lack of aspiration or hubris, irrelevance or impertinence.

And stuck talking about capitalism, because the polarities of the present ideology of doing nothing are riveted to it. On the one hand, lifestyle suggestions for doing less, forms of capitalism tweaked with wellness to make them more humane; on the other, political manifestos seeking the abolition of capitalism altogether. Present forms of doing nothing can neither imagine life existing beyond it nor conceive humans facing any problem apart from it — as if only capitalism keeps us from luxuriating innocently in life on Earth. But once I acknowledged that I was doing nothing, I also had to acknowledge that superseding capitalism would still leave me existentially screwed. I do not argue against working for capitalism's dismantlement. I am not indulging in an entitled invitation to despair, decadent quietism, a conservative rejection of change, or morbid belief that the only valid response to life is to lie down and die. I merely assert that the effectivity of such endeavors will distort as long as they deny their nonnegotiable framing realities. And it is for this reason that I dwell so extensively on such issues in this book. Worthy or incontestable as anti-capitalist endeavors may be, as long as they are fueled by existential denials, it will be difficult to discern whether they are being performed to achieve their purported goal, or the purported goal is an unconscious ruse to engage in activities that, being all too easily self-validating, easily distract from the intransigent, unavoidable malfunctions that indelibly stain any human life. We will be doing something merely to avoid acknowledging where nothing can be done.

So why should you bother practicing doing nothing? Quite simply, because you have no choice. Meaning that doing nothing is a rather strange kind of practice. I was hesitant to take up the invitation to write about it. And reading back over what I've written has not always been easy. There is something embarrassing about having authored a book that takes next to no pleasure in the fact that most people's practices are attractive precisely because people have chosen to do them. But doing nothing entered my life from other sources than the heroics of choice. It came into being from the confrontation with limits, boundaries, and defining perimeters. It has been the shadow side of my attempts to use decisions to mold the shape my life has taken. It is what I have had to do when my path through life was blocked by structures and conditions that could not be changed. It is how I carried on once I crashed my car into the brick wall of the nonnegotiable, how I dealt with the injuries accrued. It has qualities, therefore, of the experience of palliative care, disability, and queerness. Mournful feelings of entrapment and shame exist cheek by jowl here with the unexpected opportunities such situations afford.

It is my belief that the realization that what you have been doing all along is in part doing nothing is a realization awaiting us all. It is a constant feature of the existential backdrop of our condition that the immediate distractions of our lives keep us from confronting. As a result, very few know its ways from the start (although teenagers are bestowed with certain privileged revelations, which the slide into adulthood, as I will discuss, does much to encourage them to forget). Since there are myriad ways in which a person can land up in this place, doing nothing is therefore quite diverse, allusive, and more difficult to pinpoint than most other practices. It is as much a mood or mode in which you can find yourself doing things as it is what you find yourself doing per se. It teeters on the edge of being a pose; that is its risk. One must practice hard to keep one's balance and not fall off into being insufferable. Style is often necessary if you are to succeed; at times it is one of doing nothing's highest goals. Doing nothing flourishes when priorities shift from the pragmatic to the aesthetic.

There are a variety of different means by which we come to the realization of what we should do when there is nothing that can be done. In my own case, it was through a confrontation with mental illness. While I do not consider that this constitutes the sole route, or that grim beginnings necessitate dispiriting conclusions (this book ends with a smile), it is nevertheless relevant for understanding the character of my practice. Moreover, I hope it might offer solidarity to those out there who have suffered likewise. Because the fact that mental illness is not at all uncommon does little to compensate for its distress. And the fact that we are more prepared to acknowledge this than in the past hasn't necessarily resulted in us being any more open to listening to the truths bestowed on those in pain. People busy themselves with making one better to comfort themselves that something got done; in trying to help, they deny the reality of the very problem they are hoping to resolve. Experience has therefore taught me to distrust those who speak the language of wellness and good health. There's something they don't want to hear.

My own confrontation with doing nothing came on the heels of a particularly debilitating mental breakdown that had brought me limping and whimpering back to the therapist's office. Decades before, I watched my mother in her sixties be kicked to the ground by a series of disturbing psychotic episodes from which she never properly got back on her feet. Over the course of the following years, she barely left the house. Something small but significant in her eyes completely disappeared. It was replaced by a quiet but tangible terror that she learned to keep frozen in place with the most rigid of habits and daily rituals. Her gaze became flat, petrified, a kind of awful void, and to distract attention from this disfigurement, she started overcompensating with her facial gestures. It was as if she'd tried to relearn the basic conventions of expression by studying an illustrated how-to guide to human portraiture. Everything was right, but none of it rang true. It was uncanny. This was my mother, and I am a sissy mommy's boy. She was the center of my idea of home. But since she no longer seemed to be my mother, what was she doing in the house I grew up in? Keeping up the performance that nothing had changed became her practice; trying to be an appreciative audience to it became mine (though one at which I have rarely been successful). By the time I was pushing fifty, it had become clear to me that I would have to confront the possibility that I was going to share her fate. I needed to establish whether the ongoing disarray I experienced at an almost constant level behind the closed doors of my adult life was just a result of poor self-management—and so something that a bit of light counseling might rectify—or something more invasively broken. It was the latter. When I told the results of six months of professional psychological testing to a riotous health-care-professional friend of mind, her response was blunt: "Most people with these readings are dead or in jail."

In the years following, I have had to ease myself into understanding that while there are things that can be done to alleviate symptoms, the problem itself is never going away. It is structurally hardwired. I can rant and rave as much as I want about an appalling family inheritance, the injustice of all that it has made impossible, the basic "normal" things I have wanted to do but probably now won't, and all the rest of it. Nevertheless, I am subject to a situation that neither is of my own making nor could have been otherwise. I might learn new ways to breathe and make these cramped conditions temporarily more bearable, maybe interesting. (They have certainly informed the parade of different artistic practices I have participated in during my adult life as I searched for compensation for the home I lost, when I lost my mother, when she lost herself.) But I am never getting out. About that, there is nothing that can be done.

We work hard to avoid such revelations. And this work involves us in other ongoing and mostly unacknowledged practices, including keeping yourself busy, getting on with it, carrying on, making the most of it, putting yourself out there, trying to be the best you can, keeping your chin up, and other such modalities. I reject none of them. They sometimes offer people techniques for getting by. But they are not for everyone, and for many they are simply unavailable. This is not only because of socioeconomic concerns, or debilitating forms of mental illness, or refusal to think positively, or other typical assumptions. It is also because some people, irrespective of where they come from or find themselves in life, are marked by an ineradicable philosophical proclivity of being. This has little to do with being intelligent, smart, bookish, academic, brainy, or good at school. It has to do with being the kind of human that is incapable of not doing what a human, more so than any other animal we know, can do: thinking extensively beyond the mere pragmatic fulfillment of needs; thinking for the sake of thinking, even if it leads to destabilizing the territory on which you are trying to build your sense of home. It is a practice of truth, although easily written off as dysfunction. And so I have not always agreed to get well. It hasn't always been possible. And the can-do optimism that demands that it should is often brought at the expense of insight and, as a result, is in sore need of being provincialized. Part of me wants to see it stripped of its smug and mostly censorious assumption of universal validity and made to face the possibility that it is simply the meager worldview of a local belief system seeking to condone the hubris of its colonial ventures. I want revenge.

But the ultimate problem with the can-do worldview is that it trains us in ignoring the nonnegotiable limits of our own lives. And this has devastating effects on our ability to inhabit the nonnegotiable limits of human life as it must be lived on Earth. It makes us feel obligated to opt for too much instead of too little. When I am in one of my rare moments of trying to escape doing nothing, I find myself adopting the hubris of magnitude. I start piling up stuff (things, possessions, experiences, commitments, relationships, endeavors, worthy causes, and maybe practices, too) to blot out of sight the limits of my ability to choose what I want my life to be. It is a hoarding practice with metaphysical aspirations, its clandestine aim to erase evidence of impotence from my life. I assume if I can manage it, I will then live better. But in this life, I have found that when I keep on running, I keep on being pursued. And so doing nothing ensued when I finally stopped allowing myself to be chased. It is what happened when I no longer got away. When I admitted that life was a condition of being caught. When I couldn't make things better. When there was nothing that could be done.

The practice of doing nothing thus eclipses politics as the ultimate horizon of human endeavor. It reveals a dark surrounding penumbra that radiates out into something else. Politics, as a result, barely registers in what follows. Political action constitutes one of human life's most far-reaching practices for making change and putting faith in the hope that there is always something that can be done. Since it is almost impossible to have humans without there being politics, it is also defining of the species. But if politics is simply a fact of human life, to vaunt it above other things is to make a virtue out of a necessity. It is to confuse the ontological for the moral — as if the ineradicable fact of something in human life were proof it must be good; as if life on Earth were structured only for human flourishing rather than for no reason at all.

I have wondered if this confusion constitutes a disavowal of the fear and shame that come from realizing that politics is simply our fate. After all, if it is possible to make a virtue out of the political and view it as proof that we are rich, it is just as easy to flip the table and see the nonnegotiable political orientation of human operations as evidence of poverty. Because if politics is a participatory art of social transformation and change, then human life (a) has never yet been good enough, (b) has always therefore lacked, and (c) will continue to remain so until there are no more humans to necessitate the activity known as politics. This does not invalidate expending political effort. But it does put the self-righteousness accompanying its exercise in a questionable light; it seems like self-infantilization — a means of avoiding that we are doomed to having to change things using politics. The political in human life is thus a genuine antagonism; it is the stage on which some of the most striking performances of human agency occur, while simultaneously the slab on which such agency is repeatedly slaughtered. It is doing something while sliding around on a platform about which nothing can be done.

Politics is simply what we're stuck with. It isn't everything. It's a constituent factor of a certain middle ground of human social life and discourse production that human anxieties periodically hope will beat the surrounding competition. It's not the foundation on which everything else rests; not the base for all other superstructures. It's as much lost in space as anything else. And so, when I found that what I was doing was doing nothing, I found I no longer resided naturally in politics' domestic center. I found myself instead in polarized feral peripheries, often simultaneously, as in a holograph. I could experience being slowly crushed to death by perplexing quotidian mundanities indifferent to the political at the same time as being exposed to existential, cosmological, and even apocalyptic issues that dwarf it. It was as if the comforting opacity of the political had become transparent; I could look straight through from one side to the other. As a result, this book is bluntly divided in two to reflect the shuttling back and forth between, and harsh superimpositions of, the phenomenological realities that have constituted my life. Its first half is consumed by an unapologetic confessional mode. But in its second half this is abandoned in a sudden turn to a long close reading of Lars von Trier's 2011 *Melancholia*—a film that replicates the polarized simultaneities of doing nothing by brutally dramatizing the profound existential indifference of the cosmos through the immediate realities of human subjective life. When you find yourself doing nothing, there is no longer any padding to soften the blow between the self and the cosmos; they either grate against each other, creating a wince, or cancel each other out in disorienting lurches without transition.

Without acknowledgment of the crushing force of this polarized frame, the political withers into merely ineffective denial of human impotence and vulnerability. Those most capable of acknowledging this are therefore those caught in patterns of mental illness from which escape has become impossible;

the insight is the gift bestowed when your fate is to work out what to do when there is nothing that can be done. To understand this existential framework, you must be caught in the very subjective self-involvements that would seem to be antithetical to the political itself; depression and mental illness in those doing nothing are both method and practice for attaining truth. I therefore do not write *about* them. As I argue in part 2, to write about such things—to partake in the uncritical endeavor of conceptually clarifying merely how they should be understood—is tantamount to disbelief in their very existence; just another attempt at turning doing nothing into doing something instead. By contrast, the practice of doing nothing is a testament to how thinking happens and how the world looks *from* the perspective of such conditions. It inverts the usual assumptions that the "I" is reliant on the "we"; here it is the "we" that is reliant on the "I." Mere adaptation in the name of good health to the middle ground where the "we" resides must therefore be avoided and voided, because doing nothing is an act of solidarity and a profession of faith in the idea that if you want to know the truth, then don't get well.

Fairy tales sometimes show us that it is precisely those who remain incapable of denying their limitations who ultimately get the prize. In Hans Christian Andersen's famous story, it is because the princess continues to be bothered by the pea, even though it is buried beneath a mountain of mattresses, that she gets to marry the prince. Her unquestioning acceptance of her condition of being chronically thin-skinned is precisely the precondition of her salvation; if she could somehow have transcended her disability, the quality of her life prospects would have been less. The princess has something to teach us, then, precisely because she's sick. And in saying this, I do not deny the real miseries attendant on illness; I have too much personal experience of what they're like. But it helps to draw attention to the fact that a space exists between, on the one hand, such miseries and, on the other, the stupidity, blindness, indifference, and shortcomings of empathy that are easily produced by good health, vibrancy of the body, and a general sense of well-being. As someone who does nothing, I have had to loiter in that space. In part, for sure, because I am not well. But also out of a desire to see things that would otherwise remain concealed. Barred from the good luck that allows some to identify confidently with the choices they have made and the resulting things they have done, doing nothing lights up the potential poverty of such privilege.

ACKNOWLEDGMENTS

Writing this book has embroiled me in ironies. Because writing a book, even one as modest in proportion as *Doing Nothing*, is a lot of work. It is hardly doing nothing. Never in thirty years of publishing has such apparently small a thing cost me so much. Intense labors, seemingly endless, have been required to house-train the intensity of emotions that continue to swarm for me around the issues I address. But if it took a long time, *Doing Nothing* did at last get done. And for that I remain solely grateful to my editors at Duke University Press. To the sage and patient Elizabeth Ault and the committed and uncompromising Margret Grebowicz. More than any editors I have worked with, they gave me the time and opportunity to stagger around until I found my way. And maybe found myself, too.

All images and all artwork in the images are the author's own.

Part 1   **About Me**

NOTHING IS A BAD THING. It is a sign of privation and poverty. Old Mother Hubbard goes to the cupboard only to find that there is nothing there. As a result, her "poor doggy," man's best friend, must go hungry and Hubbard is shamefully exposed as an unfit caregiver. Nothing is the augur of a sterile future. In the opening scene of Shakespeare's eponymous play, King Lear cautions his daughter Cordelia when she will not flatter him that "nothing can come of nothing."[1] It is testament to the play's uncompromising and nonnegotiable vision that Lear's saying is the darkest form of irony. It turns out to be woefully optimistic. At the play's end, when the now decimated, broken king staggers toward the audience carrying Cordelia's dead body, we are made witness to a condition that is incomprehensibly worse. The list goes on.

Nothing is no good. It is not on the side of life. It is absence, lack, and annihilating void: emptiness instead of plenitude, lassitude instead of vigor, and despair instead of hope; indifference rather than relish, defeat rather than perseverance, and abandonment rather than care. One can recognize the presence of its magnetic force by the way in which it makes everything veer toward depletion: toward bland as opposed to tasty, mute as opposed to convivial, lazy as opposed to hard-working, vagabond as opposed to civilized, feral rather than domesticated, and black and white rather than colorful as a rainbow. It is easily suspected of favoring a monotony of the same over plurality. It has proclivities toward a grim, ashtray aesthetic, like the pointless surface of the bone-faced moon rather than the rich and intricate diversity of lush and sexy Earth; and, on a darker note, a perhaps fascist attraction to sameness rather than difference. Nothing is an impotent minimalism, stingy, mingy, chingy, scrimy, tightfisted, parsimonious, and cheap. With nothing, less is not more but even less than first you thought. Nothing makes everything contract and robs us of liberating experiences of expansiveness, like an ostentatious sourpuss cramping everyone's enjoyment at a party. It is a guaranteed disappointment of perfectly valid happy expectations. It is frigid when pleasure is on offer, lachrymose when laughter is easily in reach, and abstemious when largesse is available, acceptable, and what's called for. Nothing is no fun. Life calls for something else. Anything. Anything but nothing. *So do something!*

But I stay put. It's not even resistance. I'm just constitutionally bent toward anything that whispers sweet nothings in my ear. Like a plant turning to the light, my attention bestows itself on deserts, empty parking lots, and the sterile anonymity of airport hotel rooms entered for the first time; the apartment I have rented before I move my possessions in, struggling seaside towns off-season, back alleys absent of human traffic,

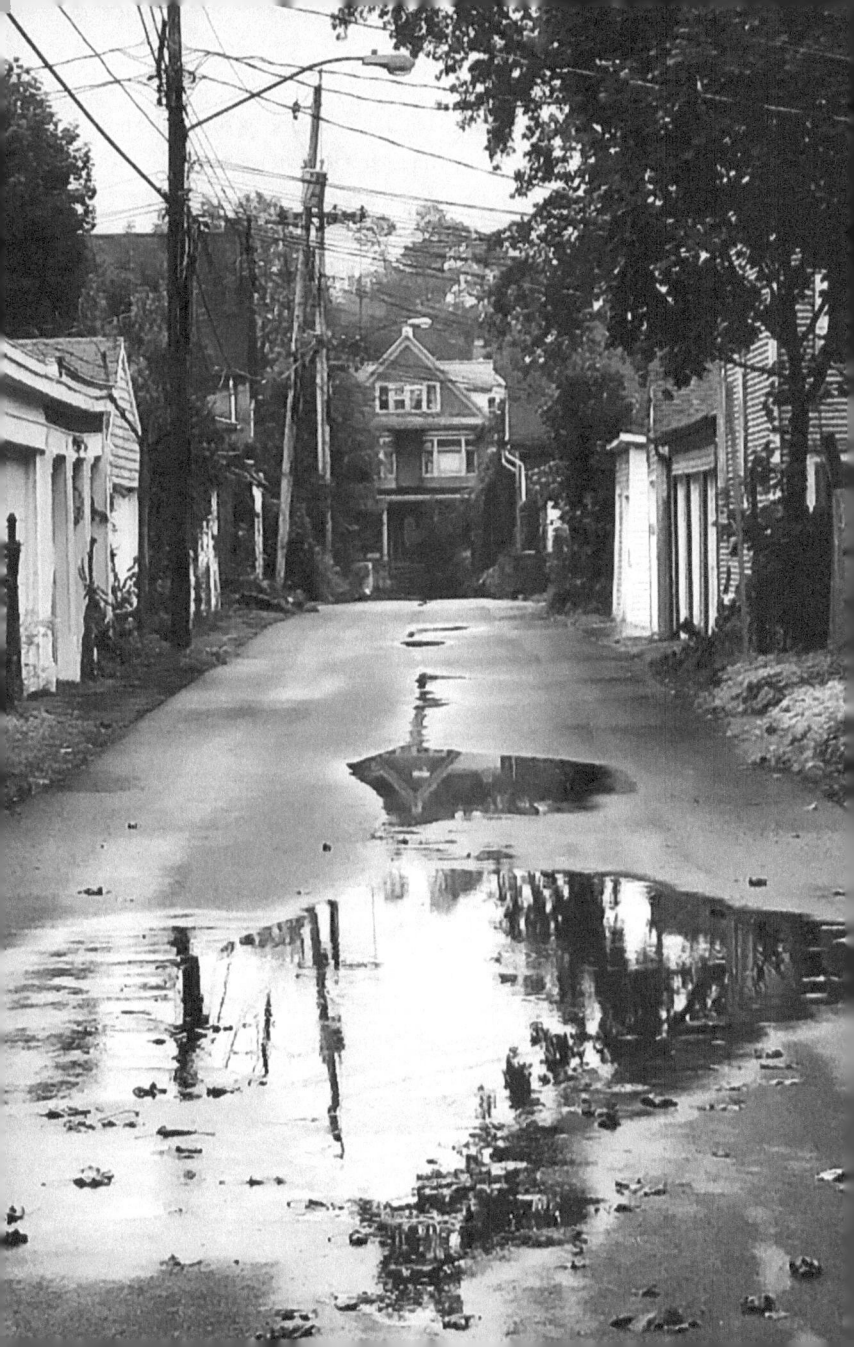

and the neither here nor there that constitutes the limbo condition of being in transit; the austerities of monastic life, the late-style feeling that things are nearly over and thus there is nothing left that one can do, and the ugly modern university campus where I work, which became like a poem to me once COVID-19 had blanched it clean of student life by herding all the students into the prison house of Zoom. I liked the grumpiness of cafés in Portugal for allowing me to smoke my head off while staring blankly into space; felt enormous gratitude to the Russian people during the mere seventy-two hours I spent in their country for temporarily relinquishing me and my facial muscles of their British proclivity for producing needy do-you-like-me smiles (an irrelevant form of etiquette east of Berlin); and hold deep affection for the city in which I have been able to live for decades, Buffalo, USA: an underpopulated, somewhat down-on-its-knees postindustrial slouch where 65 percent is often tops and one's negative emotions mostly respected as a perfectly valid response to a disappointing existence.

But what I love most is dreaming all day about sleep. When the sun at last goes down, I wake in the evening to intimations of eternal rest. I stare out the window at the fading light, relishing the prospect of yielding soon to the only satisfying lover I have ever known: my bed. After the heartache of the day, it reaches out its hand and leads me back once more toward its smiling, velvet darkness with all its sensual charms, forgetting, solace, and tear-bestrewn annihilations.

These are a few of my favorite things. Nothing is my style.

———————————

To those who conceive nothing as a bad thing, my ability to take pleasure in striking mildly pessimistic poses must be irritating. I think this is what a friend of mine felt when he was no longer able to trust the authenticity of my leitmotif: my frequent claim that, as an adept of nothing, I am not fully on the side of life. My phrase probably sounded bogus to him, like a shoddy theatrical effect. But it was well-meaning enough. The years had brought me to an almost biological understanding of my proclivities; I saw myself as a plant yearning for the fingernail sliver of the moon rather than growing as an act of worship to the life-giving sun; the tendrils of my being would wince and recoil vampire-like from invitations to feast at life's brightly lit table. Opportunities passed by me like dishes in conveyer-belt promenade in a sushi bar—jobs, sexual encounters, other delicacies from the big wide world—yet I rarely felt comfortable snatching for the goods. On the rare occasions I did, the pretty food would end up ruined on the floor, and I would be left with my endeavors laughing in my face. I therefore stopped perceiving myself pathologically (as a person sick with nothing who must be cured) and took to conceptualizing within a more nonnegotiable frame. Implacable, incurable, and indifferent to treatment, I am therefore not fully on the side of life. My leitmotif is simply how I have tried to inhabit this fact.

Such acceptance has sometimes felt good. Which makes sense. Acceptance requires we cease bothering the world; it is a highly respectable form of doing nothing. For example, I am presently crawling through middle age. Looking back over the years traversed I easily trace undulating patterns made from the piles of broken dreams. It is tempting to keep my face fixed toward the future by riveting it in place with a nonnegotiable smile. Looking back, after all, can be a risky business. When Orpheus falls prey to the temptation, he consigns Eurydice permanently to death; when Lot's wife casts her gaze back upon the city of Sodom, she is transformed into a pillar of salt. But when I turn and look the Gorgon in the face, I find we're smiling at each other. It transpires that by doing nothing I have been as much preserving aesthetic values I am loath to betray as belligerently upholding fidelity to my miserable cause. It's not fear that's to be found in a handful of dust; it's beauty.

Nevertheless, confident claims that I am not fully on the side of life have had their wobbly moments. During the early days of the COVID-19 pandemic, for example, I became, like everyone else, obsessively preoccupied with hygiene and safety. My skeptical friend opined that this looked like craven self-interest in preserving my own life. His eyebrows would hover ironically as I quizzed him about where he had managed to find a particular kind of bleach spray and how he had worked out that this should be the favored option, or whether he thought it necessary to disinfect his house keys once he'd come back from shopping, or what was the official word on whether fabric face masks were a good idea or not. The looming conclusion was that I lacked the guts to follow through from theory to practice. And this caught me in a conflict of interests. By doing nothing to protect myself from infection I could easily have remained congruent with my self-identification as someone not fully on the side of life. This would have confused me with those convinced the pandemic was simply a means of big government exerting covert infringements on civil liberties; all I would have needed to complete the look was a red MAGA baseball cap. But I am not a Trump supporter, nor did I have a problem doing what the authorities asked of me in a time of national and global crisis. Fidelity to doing nothing thus identified me with those whose politics I didn't share and made me questionable to those whose politics are roughly my own. Not for the first time, I found myself in a political no-man's-land between misrecognition and rejection. Advantageous was the opportunity it afforded to inhabit inevitable questions attendant on the political rather than having to participate in the implementation of answers. But within the desperation and urgency defining life within the ongoing and constitutive crises of the present historical moment, it has remained difficult to avoid acknowledging how easily this seems questionable. Surely one should be doing something instead. *So do something!*

Our modern predicaments have been so pressing that political activists have sometimes found themselves employing the very doing nothing one would expect them to abhor. Some of the most famous acts of modern political dissent have been constituted by active forms of nonaction. Instances include hunger strikes such as the 1981 Irish hunger strike, which helped pave the way to a radical Irish nationalist politics and to the transformation of Sinn Féin into a mainstream political party; and Mahatma Gandhi's repeated employment of protest fasting, which helped, among other things, to enable mill workers in Ahmedabad to win a pay rise (1918), to force the British government to withdraw certain clauses from its controversial Community Award (1932)—which Gandhi believed would destroy the unity of Hindu society—and to attempt to create (in 1924 and 1947) Hindu-Muslim unity. One could also note the long history of sit-ins, from the lunch counter sit-ins during the civil rights movement, to John Lennon and Yoko Ono's two 1969 bed-ins for peace, through to the 2016 US House of Representatives sit-in in which members of the House Democratic Caucus protested against the Republican Speaker, Paul Ryan, to be allowed to vote on gun control legislation in the aftermath of the June 12, 2016, Orlando nightclub shooting. Strategically appropriated for moments of crisis, forms of not doing can be recast as negation: their indifference redeemed as concern, their lassitude transfigured into dogged intransigence and deliberate obstruction.

In an act of comradeship with such strategic politics, theoretical discourse has expanded its purview to include reflection on similarly paradoxical modes. For example, a small intellectual industry has developed in praise of Bartleby, the main character of Herman Melville's oft-cited 1856 short story "Bartleby, the Scrivener: A Story of Wall Street." To all demands and orders from his employers, Bartleby famously answers merely with "I would prefer not to." Doing nothing means that Bartleby does not budge. Quite literally. He must ultimately be removed by the police from the office building in which he has been squatting and is taken to jail, where he refuses to eat and eventually dies—a hunger striker to a cause he does nothing to articulate. He therefore exits human life a mystery: uncompromisingly indifferent to clarifying forms of self-expression. But one senses that Bartleby will haunt the narrator, the elderly lawyer and Bartleby's former boss, for the rest of his life. He might even project him into activism, because the lawyer's last words are "Ah Bartleby! Ah humanity!" It is a cri de coeur, lighting up the landscape of incomprehension and despair with a momentary flash of utopian sensibility. And it is also inscrutable, as if we were witnessing the narrator transforming into a Bartleby of the future—one who will answer all demands, henceforth, with "Ah humanity."[2]

Bartleby unleashes a virus. By doing nothing, he lodges himself permanently in the mind of another and changes the course of history. Lacking in any clear affective markers of fidelity to a cause, he is nevertheless unambiguously committed. It's just that his mode of commitment is so staggeringly circumscribed and literal-minded, it verges on stupidity. Like a postwar experimental artist, Bartleby relinquishes all other decisions except to follow one self-imposed law to the bitter end. The Japanese conceptual artist On Kawara in his famous *Today* series created nearly three thousand paintings, all in accordance with nonnegotiable instructions: that he would paint the name of the date on which he was painting the name of the date; that if the painting could not be finished on that date, it would be destroyed; and that the series would continue until his death. Bartleby is therefore a Fluxus artist avant la lettre, activating his agency to submit to conditions in which his agency will no longer function. The aim is to see what happens. Everything about it is legible. There is therefore no mystery at all. The fascination he continues to inspire is simply evidence that the joke is on us.

The case of Bartleby and the appreciation he inspires suggests that if doing nothing is mostly frowned on, exceptions will be made when the decision to do so expresses unwavering conviction. I wonder, then, if the disapproval directed at me by my detractors is just an attempt at ascertaining whether I'm capable of plucking something out heroically from the vast swarm of possibilities and holding it dear. Anything will do, even the very nonactivity of doing nothing that's seemingly got their goat. Hurtful as they have often been—and usually under the bogus camouflage of political critique—I nevertheless entertain the possibility that it was all just a perverse expression of a desire for me to be someone who could desire. For me to be someone who could condense my tastes into a beam of light to pinpoint something singular. (Or fear of what I might be if I don't.) Because if there are still people who can make strong choices, there is still hope that we might be loved. And maybe that's what bothered my friend during the pandemic. If I could have been more flagrantly committed to being purportedly not on the side of life, it would have proved I was mature enough to love. And love him. Which I did. But no. Not enough to want to be dead. And so there's nothing now that can be done. Since obviously I remained alive.

All that's left is to broaden the issue out, bring thought to bear on the matter, and question whether choice can ever be so cut and dry. It is of course easy to see why we might want choice to be performed with conviction. Strong choices are attractive. However grand or modest, they are convincing evidence that someone has taken the risk of confronting their lives as a project whose shape results from the decisions they have made to mold it. They are the living proof of the powers of human agency. During the distressing times when I have found it hard to accept that doing nothing is my fate, the strong choices of others have sometimes offered themselves to me to inspire hope that I might live better. I have been turned on by the impression that those who make strong choices know who they are and where they want to be in life, and I have imagined that if I hang around them and their stories, the effects will rub off and I'll gain such clarification for myself. As a result, I have struggled throughout my life with an addiction to gorging on the biographies and autobiographies of those who I imagine have got the whole "how to live" question sorted out. Certain seductive heroics linger at the peripheries as I nestle down in my comfy chair to read about what these people have been up to. And it could be argued that living vicariously in this way is commensurate with doing nothing. Because it is a means of outsourcing to someone else the labor involved in having a life.

But ultimately it is a form of bad faith, one in which doing nothing becomes a kind of Loserdom to which those who consider their lives shamefully lacking can banish themselves. And this makes acknowledging doing nothing a hard sell in our contemporary world. Because the pervasive sense of anxious precarity has made many of us more than willing to cave in to the pressure to curate suspiciously overcoherent profiles of ourselves and our professional identities so that, purportedly, we can circulate effectively and survive. I have therefore had to work hard at becoming instantaneously frigid when the siren calls of the narratives of others' gripping lives inspire envy to dance in the empty spaces of my soul. My aim has not been self-empowerment. I have not been trying to show the world and remind myself that doing nothing is a wonderful thing too. The fact that it's easy for me not to appreciate what I've got doesn't mean that the reality of all that is genuinely bland, monotonous, or disappointing and distressing in my life is somehow redeemed just because I have offered it the possibility of being validated—like an abused dog that has been offered a treat and now wags its tail. Neither has it been a question of self-respect. Because while doing nothing is not self-loathing, neither is it some goth remarketing of self-love. If anything, it is a kind of self-indifference, a kind of sobriety that eclipses addiction to positive judgment and self-validation and makes room as a result for truth. Because contrary to the impression given by those who have burned through life on the fuel of a singular passion, much of life does not in fact result from adamant decisions that remain binding.

Doing nothing does not, then, mean that I have never practiced anything at all. It's just that those things have tended to be more holiday romance than "till death do us part"; they were with me for a certain time only until they passed into different stories that no longer included me. Things ultimately slipped through my fingers. There was little I could do. Desire came and went. In my childhood and adolescence, for example, I was consumed by the desire to play the viola. I remember the first time I had the chance to pick up an instrument and place it under my chin. I felt like I had arrived. (The only other time that has ever felt so much like something was waiting for me was when I got to place a cigarette between my fingers for the first time at the age of fifteen. I knew it was meant to be.) But by the age of twenty-two, I had quit the relationship and moved on. A whole host of forces intervened that were stronger than the glue that had attached me to the practice in the first place. The adolescent social bonds accompanying playing in youth orchestras were replaced by the grim interactions of professional life, with all their mean competitiveness, backbiting, and moaning about conductors and other colleagues. I met an extraordinary pack of friends and felt that being with them was ultimately a better use of my time than hours spent alone in a practice room or rehearsing with people I no longer particularly liked. The strange and often unacknowledged erotics of academic life started to compete for my attention: the luxurious onanism of sitting in a library immersed in a book with a pencil in my hand; the peculiar temporal suspension attendant on entering the writing zone; the unexpected performative euphoria of teaching. And finally, there was the arrival of my family inheritance: a life rich with poor mental health. The psychic creatures who until then had been but sounds heard periodically from the depths of the woods at night started brazenly entering in daylight hours the clearing I had been making for myself. And they made it perfectly clear they had no intention of returning to where they came from. It has, as a result, been a cluttered life. I have had to move around in cramped conditions. Maybe I didn't have enough faith. Maybe I didn't ultimately care about music. Maybe. But once I put it down, I never once picked up the viola again. It is somewhere in my parents' house four thousand miles away. Covered in dust. As are now my parents and perhaps everything else that once attached me to that place and made it easy to call it home.

From the perspective of being able to explain who I am, giving up the viola may not have been the best of decisions. When people find out I gave it up to become an academic, they are disappointed. When I then tell them that as an academic, I also have no coherent focus (having written about a host of often unrelated things) and that as an artist I have subsequently passed through writing poetry, being a performance artist, producing installation art, and making large series of works on paper, they start looking uncomfortable. It is as if I smell bad and they were trying to extricate themselves from the stench without being so impolite as to tell me I stink. They don't know what to do with me. And so, because I like talking to people, I tend to just talk about them instead. (Not being particularly coherent means I have developed good skills at understanding what other people are about; doing nothing is probably a good prerequisite for becoming a therapist.) But the compliment is infrequently returned. And so I have had to find friendship instead in the stories of those who have known when to hang stuff up, such as the composers Aaron Copland, Jean Sibelius, and Gioachino Rossini, who all basically stopped producing long before their ends. Copland's inspiration dried up thirty years before he died, and he turned to conducting; Sibelius felt like he'd written as well as he could, burned his remaining manuscripts, and was then, according to his wife, in a much better mood for his last thirty years; and Rossini, having accumulated significant wealth from his years of success as an opera composer, basically took up good living for four decades. In none of these instances did the waning of an epoch in which significant things had been accomplished result in the expected concomitant sense of depletion of good spirits. And there is wisdom in this. Because burning up your energies on the singularity of a passion or practice could just as easily leave you abandoned at the side of the road of life—a smoking piece of charcoal, an empty gas tank, and only your rotting desires for company. Being someone doing nothing, I am not attracted by such tales of self-immolation.

If the Buddhists and Taoists are right, and change is of the essence, then moving on from one thing to another is less a sign I lack fidelity, or am unable to commit, or have an absence of staying power; it means I am in tune with the universe. To those who seem hell bent on using the strength of their choices to become singularly identifiable, I therefore wonder what it is about the universe they are seeking to avoid. It is a question to which I will return extensively later. Most people I meet seem to take for granted that cultivating their singularity is what we have been put on Earth to do. And much common lore of the cultures of North America, where I reside, assumes that a strong sense of who we are, in and of ourselves, is the best means of getting ahead and protecting ourselves from the difficulties of life. The fact that such assumptions stand up poorly to scrutiny is moot; any thug if sexy enough is pardoned for their crimes, and so handsome self-assertion gets passed off as a heroic wager placed on pragmatism. The risk we take of becoming drunk on our own self-inflation is quickly excused if it seemingly allows for the sobriety of survival. Life at all costs: difficult to argue with and easy fodder for concluding that I have failed to make binding choices because I'm either ill (and should try to get better) or criminally inclined (and should be disciplined accordingly).

But as I have said, while I am not exactly on the side of life, neither do I relish the prospect of being dead. I have been plagued by forces that have derailed my attempts to choose things to glue me to existence; and yet here I am, frequently unstuck but still willing to be alive. It is a strange no-man's-land to inhabit. I could make an analogy here with nationality and note that not being on the side of one's country of citizenship does not mean one is a traitor or terrorist. Perhaps you simply have no opportunity to live elsewhere. Why should that necessitate you feeling happy about the situation? Commitment and certainty are not the only justifications for remaining in place. Perhaps you are lingering out of a taste for ambiguities. Perhaps inhabiting questions rather than living out preordained answers is what enables you to get by and accept life. Certainly, we need to make ourselves a little richer in prepositions when it comes to evaluating allegiances. If I am not exactly on the side of life, maybe I am to the side, or above, or below; or undetectable because fully interred within; or half in and half out of it, lodged in deep at the head and shoulders but with my torso, legs, and feet gently flapping about in undulating patterns outside, like strands of sea kelp amid the green musculature of the currents of the deep.

Doing nothing is therefore an opportunity for practicing a diversity of alternative distances and spatial positions in relationship to the significant points of reference in our lives. For a life outside of either/or and for or against. Even in relationship to life itself. It is to live with a clear understanding that the forces around us can easily detach us from the practices we have employed to keep connected to existence, and doubling down to make sure this doesn't happen might be the means of living worse rather than better. To speak in favor of doing nothing is therefore to live against a singular rhetoric of affiliation. It is to support a democracy of intensities for the modes by which we inhabit our attachments, and the possibilities that might ensue when humans are finally entitled to do so without shame.

During the early days of the COVID-19 pandemic, I was neurotically preoccupied with questions of hygiene and safety. Like everyone else, I didn't relish the prospect of ending up looking

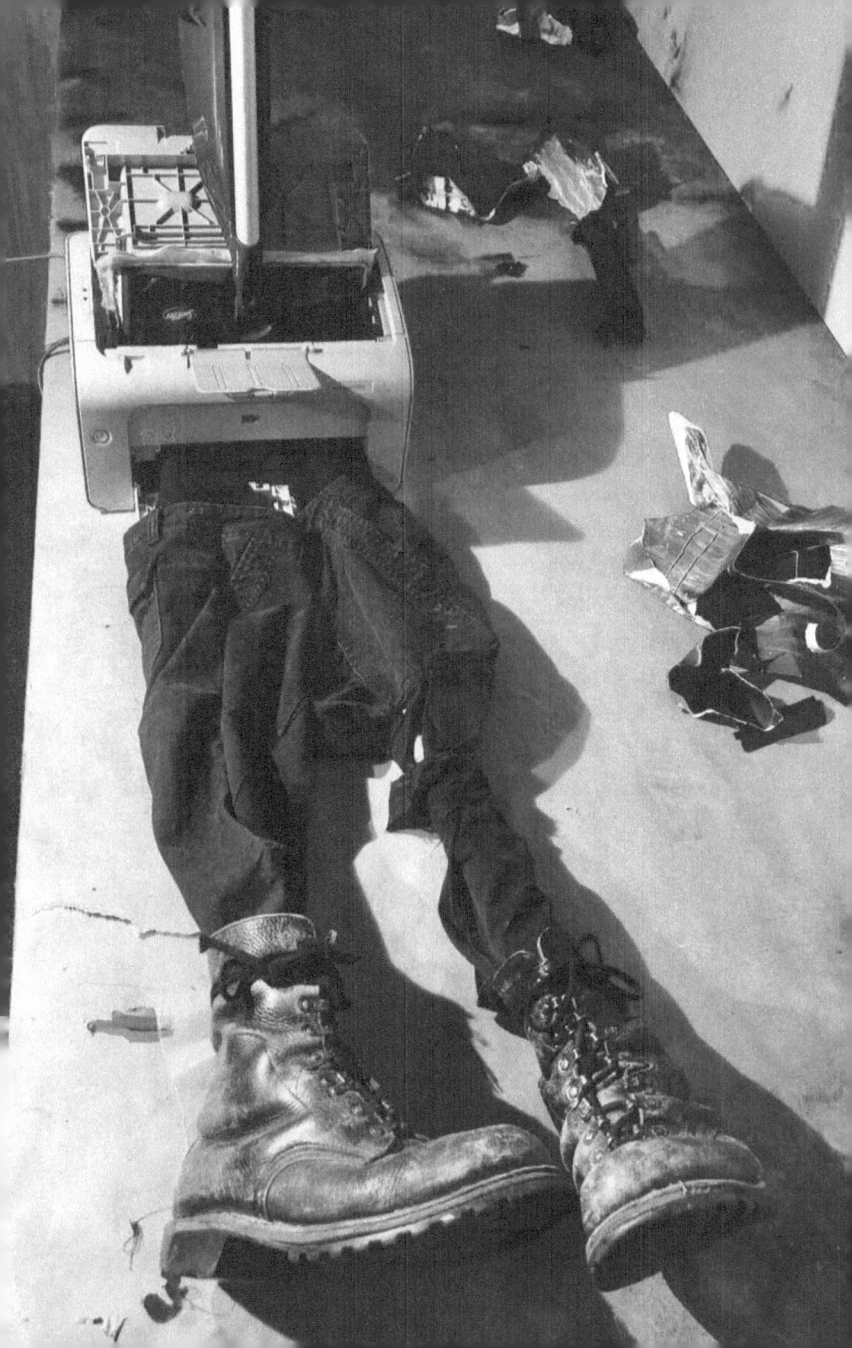

like John Hurt in *Alien* and dying a nasty, lonely death with a monstrous ventilator mask sucking on my face. But it also resulted from my long-held fear that I'm not a proper adult. Indeed, for the past thirty years I have mostly felt like I'm in bad drag as someone my own age but failing to pass. It hasn't helped my self-confidence. There has been my repeated inability to get my head around how one goes about owning property, or how to get the paperwork in order to start learning how to drive (which, at the age of fifty-four, I still haven't managed), or why my phone plan costs twice as much as everyone else's, or how to access my retirement plan, or what my social security prospects are. It has warped the basic forms of competency that would clarify the exact terms of my employment contract and what I am entitled to; much to the exasperation of those genuinely concerned about the disproportionate degrees of distress my job frequently inspires, I am constantly being taken advantage of and getting screwed over at work. It has even left me unable to establish the date in my neighborhood for "Big Trash Day." Because of this ineptitude, the secondhand fake wicker love seat—an uncomfortable item that refused to live up to its pastoral potential—continues to shed its plastic strands quietly in the entrance hall to my rented apartment. Bereft of ambition, it can now aspire only to the half-hearted pretense of being a dead houseplant. I have resigned myself to the fact that it will never make it into the Leviathan digestive tract of the garbage truck.

During the pandemic I was convinced that because my neighbors were proper adults, they must know whether, for example, to spray that can of chickpeas or bag of carrots with bleach solution before putting it away. They knew their duty and were working to guarantee their survival of the coming apocalypse, whereas I had little to no idea. Far from hoping to die, I felt embarrassed that someone might find out the meager care I was prepared to bestow on trying to keep myself alive. I therefore kept up the pretense of asking relevant practical questions. And from this I realized that if I was going to come out as someone doing nothing, I would need steely nerves. All too easily, doing nothing—suspended as it is between the get-up-and-go of *la vita activa* and the got-up-and-gone of death—leaves damning evidence, like the silver slime of a snail, that you have let yourself go and lack the requisite instincts for self-preservation.

Because of my inability to fully master the protocols of pandemic food hygiene, comestibles and other goods started lining up on the staircase outside the door to my apartment. They looked like refugees sitting in government buildings, waiting to see if their papers would be approved. The desperate had made their way to the front of the queue. Terrified packs of butter, cartons of milk, and cuts of meat huddled together for cold on the top step, dreaming of the fridges and freezers that had once been their homes. Immediately below, with a weak stoicism, crowns of broccoli slowly lost their verve as they began to wilt and faint onto the odd flaggingly optimistic orange or grapefruit. Canned goods, the marines of the group, kept a stiff upper lip on step number three; if they had thoughts or memories of the warm maternal embrace of kitchen cupboards, they were not letting on. Bringing up the rear, scouring powder and bottles of hand soap settled into a forty-foot stare; they looked like exhausted workers for Médecins Sans Frontièrs taking a smoke break in a war zone. Embarrassed, we would try not to catch each other's eye as I emerged armed with face mask and hand sanitizer and when I returned later, shattered, from my missions into the land of the infected. And in the meantime, my skeptical friend ruminated on my behavior and left. As a result of his decision, I either got my heart's desire (nothing) or was simply forced to put my money where my mouth is. Both outcomes accommodated weeping, making it difficult to see through the rain-drenched windscreen whether I was doing OK or just inconceivably bereft. Being in attendance of this ambiguity continued to seem more consistent with doing nothing than striving for clarification. In the wake of his departure, I therefore resisted the temptation to evaluate conclusively, seek revenge, bemoan the repercussions of my pretentious delusions, or regret the errors of my ways. Doing nothing required me to practice an ethics of restraint and pause on the cusp of either celebration or condemnation. He had reasons for leaving, which I respect. Considering the circumstances, I would probably have left me too.

Nevertheless, if I inhabit a sometimes-clement sense of resignation about my unimpressive track record, I do periodically make the effort at getting certified in adult know-how. With a spring in my step, full of vim and vigor, I enter the woods like the hero of my own little bildungsroman, bindle stick over my shoulder and a mind open to the possibilities of self-improvement. But I get distracted by the seductive qualities of pointless side turnings, or the footpath marked on the official map dries up, as if the powers that be have spotted my alien status on the radar and forestalled further progress. Instead of being welcomed into the warm embrace of the adult world, I find myself frightened and alone in the middle of the woods. I'm like the archetypal child of many a fairy tale. The resulting horror is less what's coming to get me; it's more the realization that I'm already caught. The approaching monster crashing through the undergrowth is simply the nonnegotiable coordinates of myself, a return of what I've always basically known: that this is my fate.

Which all sounds a little hammy: self as fate (the shoddy stage paint of amateur dramatics); there's nothing that can be done (the cry of all aped tragic grandeur). All so much easier than confrontation with a messy world where we must try our best and suffer the consequences of where that lands, however short of the hoped-for mark. I have wanted doing nothing to mean something grand. And yet there it was, as long as my arm and highly seasoned to boot: the official diagnosis of my poor, disturbed, bruised little mind, chugging out into the printer tray after six months of professional testing. No meaning at all. Not even a total absence of meaning, which at least would allow me to gnash my teeth, pull out my hair, and beat my breast. Just old-fashioned mental illness. Try to get better, Buddy! Good luck!

But I am tired of keeping faith as yet another honeymoon with yet another therapist fades yet again into the quotidian circuits of a marriage that's going nowhere. Like someone in an abusive relationship, I have become skeptical of overtures to optimism being on eternal replay (because I know the operas that follow, and they don't end well for the prima donna). Of course, my resulting futility is exasperating. But it's not that I'm not trying; it's that I'm crippled from the monotony of doing nothing but. Doing nothing presents itself to me, therefore, as an inventive if rather desperate form of pragmatism: to save me from dying from the boredom of being in pain. Because if you can't bear where you are (and I can't), and yet however hard you seem to try there's no option for going anywhere else (and in thirty years of trying, I haven't found one), what else are you going to do?

Doing nothing is therefore what I have done when I could do nothing else. It is why I wrote this little book. Writing offered me room to breathe within an otherwise intractable discomfort from which exit had become impossible. Like a Medusa, it allowed me temporarily to freeze my situation in place within the beam of my mind's eye; to turn it around, dissect, caress, embrace, and even abuse it (for revenge is sometimes necessary); to take momentary pleasure from hanging my quarry like a trophy on the wall of my soul. Writing has been a trick, low-grade magic, more a blush that comes and goes than an act that changes the external reality of my condition. (Because magic cannot change the cosmos; it merely buys us time from being solely at its mercy.) Through writing I have therefore learned the art of inhabiting my fate and making my peace with the fact that in this life I'm probably not going to get much else done. Like doing nothing, it has allowed me to live.

In my fantasy world, the ideal adept at doing nothing is someone who leaves no trace, product, explanation, testament, or profile. They are so free of the narcissism that seduces most of us at some point onto the stage of discursive and social recognition, their egos have dissolved into some other condition beyond the parameters of recognizable human life. If I were closer to my ideal, I would teeter on the edge of nonexistence, like a saint, mystic, hermit, or those adroit at asceses—fasting, meditating, praying, and moving without ostentation through the bland routines of a spartan existence in huts in the desert, caves in the mountains, and the hollows of ancient trees in the unfrequented depths of forests and woods. I would be a vampiric being, casting not even the temporary phenomenon of a shadow. Inducted into the Doing Nothing Hall of Fame, I would immediately become invisible, inaudible, and completely absent from the historical record. My very presence would disenable recording devices as I pass by them; there would be nothing but the hum of blank tape when the authorities came to play back the evidence. I daydream about hordes of surveillance perverts desiring me as their prized trophy, with my head on the wall above the fireplace so that they can keep an eye on me. But like some Cold War antihero I keep my eye on the prize (on nothing) and elude entrapment by becoming like a mirror without warp or evidence of desilvering. The surface of my being is now so polished, it merely repeats what it is placed before. And camouflaged behind the reflection of everything else, I finally feel safe. By doing nothing I have become nothing. So much so, there is nothing more to see. For the rest of my life, I will drift without fear of ever again having to cringe and squirm under the critical gaze of others.

Which is not to say that as nothing I couldn't be useful. If I could purify myself sufficiently, my skills could be put to good use in espionage or detective work, or as an assassin. De rigueur for success in these professions is an impressive lack of taste for the narcissistic gratification of being validated publicly for doing your job. But as the memoirs of spies attest, residual tendencies to self-aggrandizement can sabotage even these most pure of practitioners. All too easily, the price they pay for relinquishment of public recognition is compensated for by the covert pleasure taken in watching themselves in the private theater of their own self-reflections; even before being publicly unmasked, they appear there as those who have done things on which the fate of civilizations depends. Their self-effacement is therefore but a mask for grotesque degrees of self-importance and rabid belief in getting stuff done; it is the decorum of a clandestine elect, a secret aristocracy of those who really get to experience doing something. Kim Philby, Guy Burgess, and other members of the Cambridge Five—the famous British spy ring who worked various double-agent maneuvers for the Soviets during the Second World War and the early years of the Cold War—would epitomize such an invisible elite. Svelte of character in public, they privately binged on the unquestioned assumption of their own stature. Eminently qualified in terms of skills, they ultimately did not have what it takes. Because doing nothing is identified not only by absence of action but also by action purified of intent. It is something performed tautologically, for the mere sake of performing it. Within the psychic economy, it gets nothing else done.

Take, for example, Jef Costello, the professional hitman and lead character of Jean-Pierre Melville's pitch-perfect 1967 neo-noir crime thriller *Le Samouraï*. The action of the film concerns how the police slowly focus in on identifying Costello as the contract killer of a nightclub owner, then corner him and shoot him dead (although it transpires that Costello lets this happen). The film's sophistication lies in how our sympathies lie with Costello; we yearn for him to elude the law. Its genius lies in the fact that our allegiances are guaranteed even though we know nothing of who Costello is—of what motivates him, what circumstances led him to this line of work, or what he gains from such employment. The film thus gives the lie to the glib assumption that it is only through knowledge that we come to empathize with others. The almost inhuman absence of expression characterizing Alain Delon's extraordinary performance in the lead role is a barrier through which no personal content escapes. However far we penetrate his intimate life, nothing about him is to be found. The film's most memorable image, and perhaps its central metaphor, is therefore the rented apartment in which Costello periodically lives. Clean but shabby, it is void of incriminating evidence of Costello's identity, an almost completely empty space. The only noteworthy inhabitant (sentient or otherwise) is the small bird Costello keeps in a cage. Scrupulously, Costello feeds and looks after it, but with no visible sentimentality or anthropomorphic delusion. It is as if Costello's true desire is simply to pass over into this nonhuman life and disappear altogether. Maybe, like me, he's searching for safety too. Who knows? He disappears from life before we find out.

Irrespective, I have written a little book (which constitutes the embarrassment of having done something) with flagrant autobiographical proclivities (thus failing to meet my defining criteria of self-erasure), and I have also not been pure enough in intent to have tried to write something thoroughly useless (which at least would have been to show willing). Have I then failed? To be honest, I have no idea, and writing *Doing Nothing* has done little to help me answer. Which I guess is a kind of success. Nevertheless, it allowed me to take delight in imagining my doing nothing heroes as those who refuse to flinch into action at the order to get out there and get on with it. Fearlessly they accept that we are ultimately impotent in the face of the fact (a fact as blank as Jef Costello's face) that death bats last. The actions of others appear to them as but a means of erecting stuff to keep these existential truths out of sight. It is an embarrassing erection. But in their doing nothing land, limp is sexy, and nobody feels compelled to risk the hubris of tumescence. Poise is found there in a slump, and supine is the high jump of their Olympic Games.

On the rare occasions when I'm contemplating defection to the fabled kingdom of Can-Do, I can't banish the suspicion that all those layabouts in the United States of Doing Nothing might have a point. Is the happy soul sitting in meditation not getting something for nothing? And by setting forth to get stuff done, am I not setting myself up for being the dupe of unnecessary labors? It is enough to raise my ire. But my anger is just to keep at bay how terrifying I find the unemployed when I'm trying to get ahead. They blithely stroll too close to the edge of bottomless pits of inactivity, seemingly without vertigo, and I can hardly bear to watch them. Because in the mirror of their absent actions I see my image reflected as but a puny creature of impotent distraction. From there it is but a short journey to a paranoid state in which by doing nothing they invoke the impossible absences of other infinite realms. Such as the nauseating void immensities of interstellar space. I have placed my hopes on the speculative wager that being busy will purchase me an enclosure in which to dwell. But effortlessly, by doing nothing at all, these slobs import the very thing my actions seek to bar:

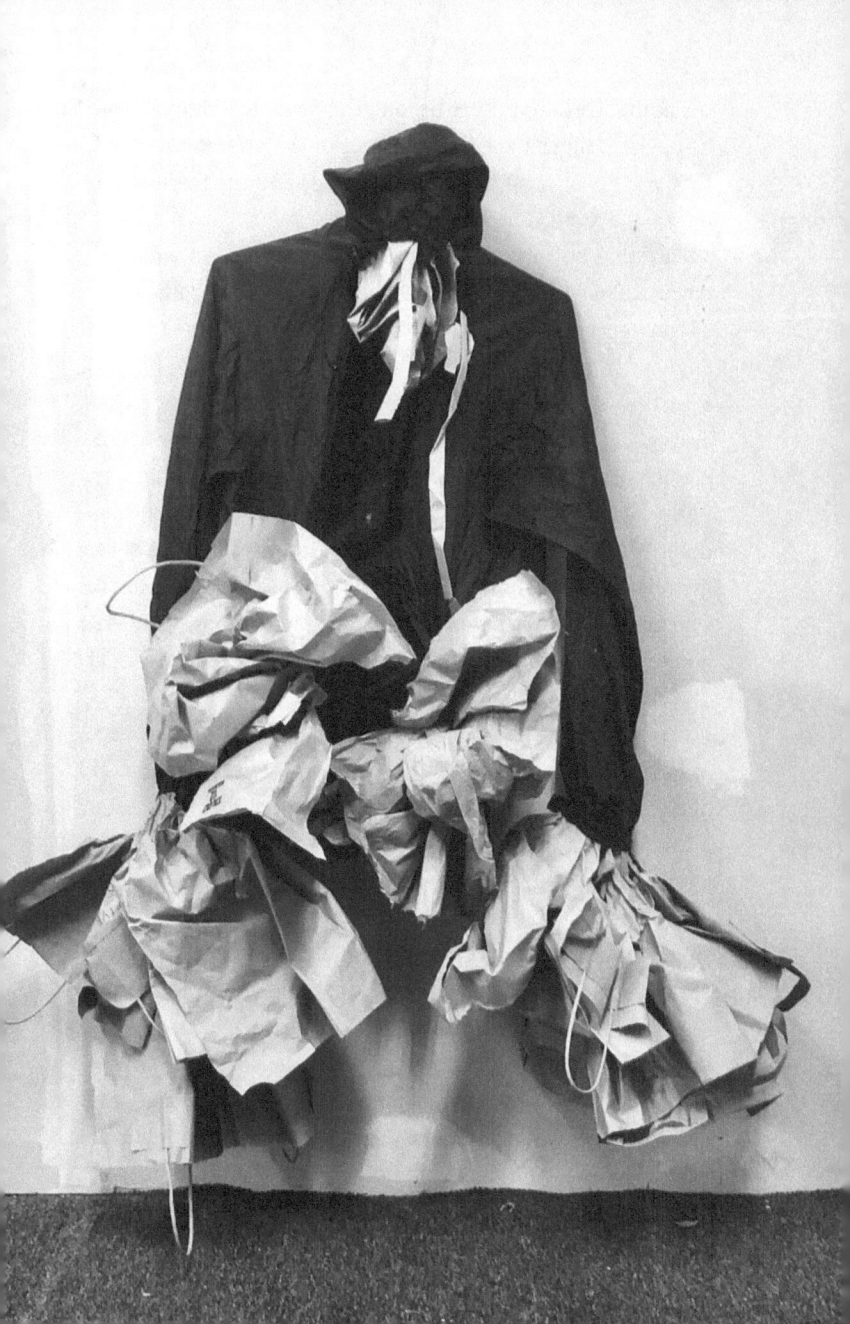

the chilly world out there beyond the door that should never be opened. Smash and grab artistes of the existential realm, they rob me of my hard-won cosmology and the foundations on which I am trying to build my home.

If doing nothing disturbs me with thoughts of what lies beyond, it also pursues me with memories lurking within. Out of the depths arise images from my past where I see myself engaged in the very inactivity from which I'm now in flight. I see a teenager luxuriating in exquisite miseries of torpor. Um-braphiliac, with the curtains closed, he lies deflated on crumpled sheets vaguely watching TV on a beautiful summer day. Parental revenants start screaming at him from the bedroom door. "*Do something!*" they demand. And in the throes of re-membering this, I flinch in recoil, as if someone were about to slap my face. But the parental ghosts are merely doppelgängers, and my recoil but the reverse of self-abuse. I am screaming at myself. I need it to stop.

I will therefore have to start identifying with the very teenage indolence that fills me with worry and rage. I need the courage of some creative rethinking. Which shouldn't be hard. After all, isn't there something magnificent about the way teen-agers uproariously refuse to catch fire in the face of adult pains to convince them that the effort is worth it? By comparison, small children seem grotesquely eager to please, annoyingly caffeinated, and too easily excited by attention. Teenagers have the nerve to limp around world-class art galleries, lame with indifference; respond at a glacial pace, and with about as much warmth, to genuine interest in their well-being; and gawp mostly joylessly into the mise en abyme of their phones. When they are in their doing nothing mode, it is difficult to believe that they are close to the peak of physical perfection. They look more like enormous broken toys whose batteries are running out, or animals cursed with being subject to an unjustly increased force of gravity. Approached from the right angle, they are an aristocracy.

Our culture drools at the lurid spectacle of adults straining to pass as youth. Standing in line at the supermarket, choruses of publications advertise hordes of Baby Jane crossbreeds and wrinkly Peter Pans who cater to this taste. Perusing these magazines, I find it easy to conclude that a defining disorder of our times must be recidivist tendencies toward slipping back into preadult life. But maybe it is the expectation of that fate that is killing us rather than the thing itself. When parents start screaming, *"Do something!"* at their teenage offspring, is it simply evidence of the tough love needed to instigate the necessary boot camp for their soon-to-be adults? Or projectional disavowal? Are the parents not haunted by the insomniac efforts they have required of themselves to retain sovereignty over their brittle adult selves? Likewise, when I take pleasure in laughing at mothers dressed like their teenage daughters and acting like their best friends, or long-in-the-tooth Hollywood actors with cheeks swollen high into marble-smooth domes of Botox, am I merely being entertained by the grotesque? Or am I not expressing relief at having been spared such ignominy myself? Perhaps these monsters should be thanked rather than ridiculed. By living out publicly their unsavory roles, they allow me the possibility of conning myself that I, by contrast, am the real thing: a bona fide adult. It is like the middle-aged social media practice of posting evidence of embarrassing teenage sartorial experiments. The adult wisdom of my generation shakes its head indulgently online at galleries of frosted blue eye shadow, the awkward nonchalance of a studied popped collar, and the failed spiritual aspirations of a poor jewelry choice. I wore a large new age crystal when I was an undergraduate and thought it beautiful. On having graduated, though, I immediately lost it running for a train. My newly conferred degree made me interpret this as a message from the universe: that it was time for me to put away such childish things. And by posting this image in middle age I am reaffirming my vows and asserting the inviolability of my adult self.

Or I'm just aping nonchalance to avoid feeling guilty for having abandoned myself. Returning to the pit in which I left myself to die, standing on the edge, I strike a pose to prove to myself and others that maturity has cleansed me of the vertigo of regret. But ultimately my posturing cannot compete with the siren song of social suicide. So I throw myself off and fall to my death. The tyrant that kept me from my true desires was simply my adult self. To enact retribution, I must therefore suffer the shame of assuming my teenage doing nothing look once more; it is why I embarrassingly exposed myself by writing this little book. Like Oedipus, who fully understands only once he has been shown to be shamefully both adult and child (sexually active, but with his mother), or Tiresias, who comes to know the future only because of tragic drag (having been both man and woman), my act of writing has been a rite of passage in which the pretentions of my adult poise have been made to curdle on contact with the embarrassments of my resuscitated teenage pose. The resulting act of self-exposing narcissistic wounding—before my editors, anonymous reviewers, and you, my readers—is therefore the payment I have made to remember that when I was a teenager, I was not just an adult in nuce waiting to know the truth. Veering toward doing nothing I may have been, but I was also onto something.

Immured between childhood incompetence and adult autonomy, teenagers are well positioned to understand that doing nothing was not always proof of criminal intentions; in the early years of life, it was explicitly demanded of us. This is easily seen when adults take pleasure in seducing children into play by talking to them in a patronizing language frequently no longer attractive to the child. Wilier than adults are prepared to admit, children tend to go along with this to accrue whatever's necessary to fuel their addictions (for sugar, narcissistic aggrandizement, and other such fare). Perhaps they also intuit that doing so will help secure leniency from the prison guards and help them make it out of the jail of childhood dependency unscathed. They're smart; this is far from given.

Play constitutes a very real part of childhood and is one of the most touching forms of doing nothing. It also produces beneficial outcomes. But to be authentic it must first take us unawares. When we come back startled to self-consciousness, we must find ourselves already immersed in its tautological anti-economy, playing simply to play. (Otherwise, we're no different from miserable corporate team members who have dressed up their labor as fun because someone pointed a gun at their heads.) Play is not reliant, then, on a set of preexisting credentials. It's not like planning to visit a certain country and making sure you have the right visa; it's more like getting to Shangri-la—the only requisite navigation tool is the ability to stumble across something. For sure, certain hardwired pro-clivities of personality can aid or impede an individual's ability to get hoodwinked. (Being gullible can help; an overly vigilant psychological security system can be a hindrance.) But play ul-timately offers guarantees of success to nobody, and its judg-ments regarding who participates in its rituals can therefore be inscrutable. It is radically egalitarian: An angel can find it a rare experience, even when a monster is at it constantly. It is like the theological notion of grace: We have done nothing to deserve it, and to all extents and purposes it is has been bestowed on us for no good reason at all. More ontological than ethical, it is a random possibility of respite hardwired into sentient life on Earth, for human and nonhuman animals alike. As such it has considerable authority. But it can also make us anxious. Because if play necessitates no fixed credentials, it possesses the terrorist ability to strike whomever, whenever. Including our adult selves. At any moment, we might find ourselves un-expectedly doing nothing.

Protecting play from being hijacked and put to work is there-fore one of the few things I should be prepared to do something about. It is beholden to me to question the actual reach of play in childhood and speculate why adults automatically conceptualize it as innocent—which seems deeply self-serving. Even if we do believe in childhood innocence, its reign must be cruelly short; we too rapidly accrue in life a track record of selfishness and unkindness toward others for it to be otherwise. If innocence is a prerequisite for play, then barring the odd saint or ingenue, *only* very young children can participate; adult attempts must be faux-naïf. The sweetness of adult reactions to children's play is then easily just a pleasurable expression of their self-serving theoretical cynicism: Since only children are new enough to the game to be innocent, play cannot genuinely threaten adults; they are too morally besmirched. So there's nothing to fear; doing nothing doesn't stand a chance.

When I started intuiting some of this as a child, it marked the beginning of a dawning realization that I had been paying for my keep. Amid all the many touching things that were done for me—including things of great sweetness prepared with love—I was nevertheless laboring to keep the ideological checks and balances of my parents' regime in order and writing myself out of the contract that could have allowed future opportunities for doing nothing. In other words, I was working very hard indeed. The complaint is not that I had to do something as a child instead of nothing. Far from it. As a small child, I was thrilled by the invitation to help adults with their tasks. I used to love being allowed to do the dishes. Similarly, I felt like I had died and gone to heaven when my mother showed me how to bring milk to a boil so that I could prepare her coffee; I would serve it to her beaming, as if she were Venus and I some pudgy little cupidon. If there was innocence to that time, it came from the fact that mastery and aptitude had yet to congeal into labor; adult chores could still be experienced as joy. The outrage came rather from the fact that I was doing unpaid overtime under the aegis of play. It was insulting to me that this was presented economically, as if I'd simply been enjoying childhood and to pay for the privilege must now get down to work. And so I have been crusading ever since. Doing nothing has been a kind of workers' compensation to unmask theft and reclaim what was robbed.

On the one hand, teenagers are told that they must start looking after themselves and can no longer act with the blithe irresponsibility of children (the past is over); on the other hand, they are repeatedly reminded that they may not yet act with the rights of adults (the future is not yet). Stuck in a no-man's-land between Eden and citizenship, they are ostensibly being ordered to wait and work. This is a poor nowhere for anyone to find themselves, and teenagers' characteristic retort of "what's the point?" (with accompanying shrug) to adult calls for signs of engagement is a final desperate attempt at civil behavior. Because the alternatives (fury or despair) inspire caregivers to intervene—increasing propinquity and robbing the teenager of whatever breathing room they still might have. Teenagers are therefore in possession of a profound understanding of how difficult it is to try moving around in cramped conditions. When they start doing nothing, it is therefore cause for celebration; it means they have not yet given up on their dignity, which requires a certain space in which to maneuver. I remember repeated rituals of sitting at the bus stop, smoking cigarettes, staring blankly into space, and being metaphysically unimpressed with existence. These were practices that allowed me the impression of having enough distance for a view of things broadly conceived. And since a room with a view is a luxury, studied arts of nihilism and the practice of doing nothing allowed me to assume a cosmology of my own making.

But can fidelity to this vision be sustained once youth has been superseded? Or is doing nothing only ever a stopgap en route to the better something our parents want? Teenagers may traditionally be associated with revolution, and revolution with change. But the history of revolution is as much a history of bathos arising from one set of iniquities being replaced for another; for all the upset, the balance of injustices remains the same. The radical potentialities of troubled teenage years can easily become the fertilizer for a law-abiding adult life to come (in which you will berate your teenage children for doing nothing). Stuck in a proletarian condition of youth, teenagers are thus their own bourgeois class in the making; they act out against an inhumane adult authority by doing nothing only until they have enough rights to seize power for themselves and enjoy the securities of everything that had previously raised their ire.

So maybe doing nothing and adult life are simply incommensurable. After all, if teenagers can be inspiring, they are just as easily a massive pain in the ass. And when that is the case, I no longer admire them for challenging adult ideologies but find them cringeworthy for aping them. Excruciatingly, they assume the world-weariness of those who have seen it all before; with pitiful results, they condemn everyone and their mother as "fascist." Of benefit is how this poor show as thespians reminds me how the adult I became was born of artifice: It had to be learned and rehearsed. Adolescence is a decade spent in a green room. It was where I tried on various ill-fitting costumes, such as that new age crystal I mentioned earlier. It is where I practiced using props so that my gestures would no longer seem so studied, such as learning to wield a cigarette with attractive nonchalance. It is where I stood in the wings, waiting to be called up onstage for the drama of adult life. It is where I tried to memorize my lines. And so teenage shortcomings remind me that if I want to retain my adult status, I will have to remain vigilant about keeping up practicing it. And maybe the misery of this prospect will encourage me to get back on track and start doing nothing again.

Or alternatively it will just exasperate. Most teenagers, after all, are lacking in the life experience that might authorize the kind of negative generalizations they enjoy making. They overcompensate rhetorically, resulting in a veritable deluge of groanworthy blanket condemnations made brittle from the kind of overweening confidence that is born of disavowed insecurity. The problem is not so much that teenagers are wrong. (Their mothers probably are fascists; their families, for sure, are bullshit.) It's rather that the teenager's relationship to being right is marked by a conflict of interest. If stating the truth of their negative proclamations were the sole aim, the presiding outcome would be a viral outbreak of uncontrollable anxiety; nothing any longer could be trusted to be as it appeared. But what mostly happens is that the confidence attained from being able to hear themselves articulating negative generalizations transpires to be the sought-after prize. It is a classic case of the medium being the message. Teenage proclamations are therefore more successful performatives than failed attempts at truth. They are a means of gaining pleasure from bolstering a flimsy ego. No different than the linguistic gambits of the adults they are soon to become. No different from me writing this book.

Part 2   **Cosmos**

LIKE ALL CHRONIC CONDITIONS, doing nothing takes up a lot of time. It is demanding, like a small child, needing much looking after; like a quietly malevolent parent, it never really lets you go. I suppose, then, I have been neither the best of parents nor the most obedient of children, since I still dream of respite and getting away. Of infidelities. After a difficult day doing nothing, I look forward to the possibility of seeing friends. I melt slightly at the prospect of the convivial clink of glasses at the restaurant table and faces gently rippling with expressions of mutual acknowledgment. But doing nothing finds its way. Just as I am about to walk out the door, I am compelled to check the gas stove one last time. Twenty minutes later, I am still there, riveted to the spot in tears. I can *see* that everything is off! (I touch the dials again.) I can *feel* it! (. . . and again.) I *know* it! (. . . and again.) But who am I? On what authority do I know? Doing nothing knows something beyond the brittle convictions of my human epistemology. It knows something else, about some other, more universal insecurity that no amount of empirical evidence can annul. Something cosmological. A vastness of forces that makes a mockery of my attempt to protect myself from danger and waltz off to dinner with an easy conscience. I therefore stay at home.

Doing Nothing doesn't want me too much out there in the world with others—in that middle ground between the isolation of the self and the abandonment of the cosmos. It keeps me from my friends. And so I live strangely: viewed from the world of social relations, not quite on the side of life. It's probably a mildly abusive relationship. But I remain because Doing Nothing is lonely and needs someone with whom to share what it knows. Maybe someone who's lonely too. I would be heartbroken to abandon it and, indeed, don't really want to. Because when I'm home alone with Doing Nothing, at least I don't worry that someone will catch the strain in my smile. (We know what time of day it is, Doing Nothing and me.) Even though I cherish the consolations of my social life, I fear my friends would never ask me out again if they knew what we'd been doing. So yes, it's complicated. As with all relationships, you can't have your cake and eat it. But Doing Nothing and I are more like lovers than master and slave. Ultimately, we just want to spend as much time with each other as we can.

Still, one of us needed to go out to work to put food on the table and a roof over our heads. And since Doing Nothing was fully employed being a chronic condition, and I am a bit of a floozy and like the odd affair, it was decided I would become a university professor. It's what I have been working at for the past thirty years, since Doing Nothing barged into my life. Like my social life, my life in the academy has been a respite from the truths that Doing Nothing dwells on at home while waiting for my return. It has been a distraction from reality rather than the conduit to its elucidation. It has been a zone of competence where I have been able to don a learned drag, slap on some intellectual pancake makeup, and swish into the seminar room as if I were a competent adult getting shit done. Pure escapism! I would be lying if I said I hadn't had some fun at work.

Academia is a theater where I perform a certain kind of drama rather than where truth happens; it is a sophisticated game I play rather than the real thing. If it had been the other way around, I suppose I might have written an academic book about doing nothing. I might even have tried my hand at one of those low-alcohol, academic-lite endeavors that college deans love for getting faculty noticed beyond the university—one of those "fun" books in which the author gets to show that they can be "fun too" ("just like you and me"). But even though I wrote to be broadly readable, I had no intention of making my professional expertise attractively available. Since doing nothing is my practice, it seemed appropriate for my readers to see me when I was not on the job. So I ended up writing something that could do nothing for my professional profile. Doing nothing is a fate, not a choice; its practice is completely indifferent to professional prowess. I am as much (or as little) qualified to write about it as anyone else who has found themselves caught in the conundrums of what to do when there is nothing that can be done. Distinctions between experts and amateurs are therefore moot. Even though I teach music history in a department of music, music history barely registers; even though I am an academic, I wrote according to different protocols. Anything else would have been betrayal.

Academic prose works as if in accordance with the dramatic conventions of late nineteenth-century realism and naturalism. Like the famous methods of the Russian theater director Konstantin Stanislavsky, it is like dealing with a fourth wall; the ideas and topics occur "as if" in the sequence in which they were logically thought. The stress, mess, and crippling professional abjections that go into writing such things are efficiently swept off the stage of the final product by totalitarian editing techniques—consigned to the green room or trashed. The audience (hopefully) never gets to see them. There is a strong addiction to carefully staging things so that acceptability can be passed off as dramatic coincidence; the authoritative reference "just happened" to be waiting at the junction to tell the author which direction to take, honest! Irrespective of how brutal or incendiary the material might be, or how radical the theoretical mode of understanding it, academic methodologies are therefore underwritten by old-fashioned and comforting narratives. The scholar is never allowed to appear as ultimately alone; there is always help at hand. The middle ground of the social, between the isolation of the self and the abandonment of the cosmos, prevails. As the final credits roll, the scholar stands as part of a huge community of other scholars, tirelessly listed, page after page, in the acknowledgments. As voluminous bibliographies attest, whenever the scholar got lost, shoulders were available to gift them a lift up for a better view. No one said it was going to be easy; writing academic books can be excruciating. But ultimately the job gets done and the scholar makes it home. As they must. Otherwise, no academic press would give them a contract. For while academic publishers are happy to let academics write about failure and other sister disabilities to doing nothing, the economic restraints placed on them by their academic customers make it impossible for their authors to fail in the process of trying to do so. Practices must never be taken so seriously that they contravene the conventional terms of being understood.

But with doing nothing no one is ever going to make it home. If doing nothing is an attempt to work out what to do within a set of framing coordinates about which nothing can be done, then there is nowhere to go; you can move around only within the place you already find yourself. You are both always at home and always on the move, both incarcerated and nomadically in exile; nobody gets to win because nobody gets to make it out. Doing nothing thus makes a mockery of hierarchies and our taste for teleological narratives concluding in the liberation of clarification. Which is why the temptation to write about it in an academic manner can effectively distract from its inconvenient truths, and why it would have been both crass and contradictory to have written about it in such a way. Because the rhetorical conventions of academic prose—the statement of the thesis, the placement of the work within the existing scholarship, the setting up of the framing contexts and background, the move to the validating examples, conclusions, and then final bibliographic credits—create seductive assumptions that it is always possible to find just enough critical distance to convince ourselves that we do in fact know where we are and where we are going. It would therefore have allowed readers to believe that there is something that can be done to understand doing nothing. Which means that something can be done about doing nothing. So why couldn't all those losers doing nothing do something about it too?

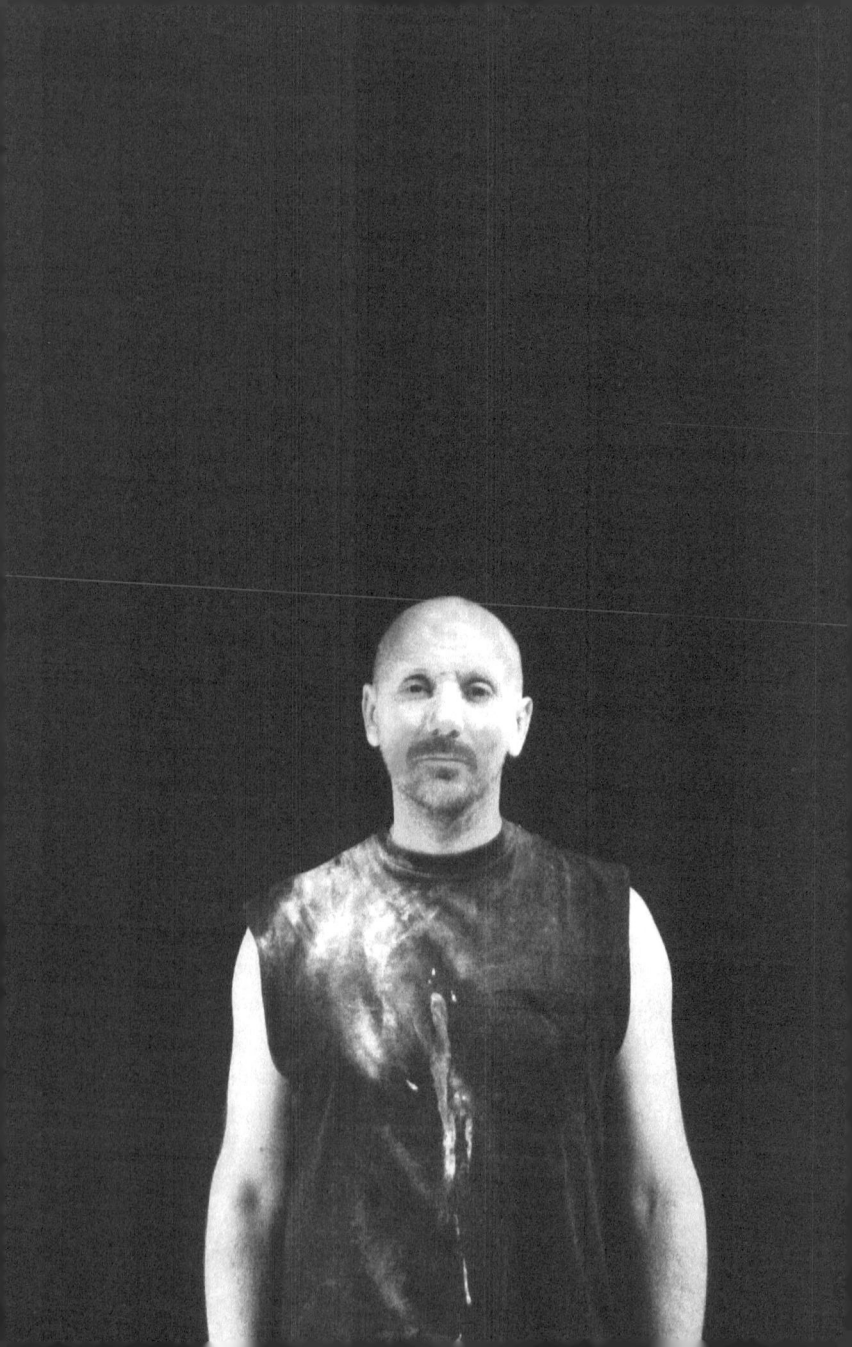

The attempt to conceptually contain doing nothing is tantamount to a statement of disbelief in its very existence. Doing nothing must therefore not be understood; it must be inhabited. But beware! Doing nothing certainly understands something about you. Indeed, doing nothing has much to say about many things and how they appear from its perspective; it is one way in which its inhabiting of itself occurs. But because the condition cannot be escaped—and so, like infinity, has no beginning or end—it moves through this process in ways that can easily seem circular, repetitive, turgid, random, strangely irrelevant, and frustratingly inconclusive. Doing nothing therefore organizes its time according to other agendas than those in which stuff gets done. And sometimes this allows one to be charmed by the unexpected things one finds oneself thinking about.

As I was writing this book, things popped up. As if from nowhere. Like meerkats suddenly standing up and looking me in the eye across the sands. Ultimately these strangers appeared only because they came from me. To be visited, I had to be blessed with an unreliable understanding of my own intentions. Only when my attention was distracted by something else did these things feel safe enough to step out from the shadows. Through distraction I created the opportunity for them to make their introductions. Because that could happen only in the clearings that opened when I was doing nothing directly in relationship to them, doing nothing was a prerequisite for making space for these others to emerge. It was an act of decorum I performed for unexpected visitations from myself.

If academic writing is like late nineteenth-century theatrical naturalism, the writing required for doing nothing is like a modernist production directed by Bertolt Brecht. Even though enormous amounts of craft must be applied, its function is to clarify rather than mask the means of production by which statements came into being. It was necessary to allow my readers to see the stagehands, the lighting equipment, and most of the set changes. By necessity, much of what got me from one stage to another remains in view. Such as the fact that I caught myself thinking about teenagers early in the writing process, amid crafting a sentence about something quite different. I'd had next to no interest in or intention of writing about them before and hadn't ever given them or their predicament much attention. But there they were. Bullies. A grubby gang of them, with their threatening scowls and flick blades, waiting to shove me off down some discursive back alley for whatever purpose they had in mind.

Even so, it didn't do me much good. Passivity may well be part of the fun of doing nothing, but in this instance my inability to stand up for myself achieved little. I was certainly enlightened and intrigued by the many things encountered from having slavishly followed these delinquents. But I remained just as much at a loss as to what I was to do once I realized there was ultimately nothing that could be done as I had been when I'd started out. And so rather than experiencing peace, certainty, or acceptance, I was plagued by a swarm of questions: What should we do when the nonnegotiable limits of our agency are made so unpalatably clear? When we are confronted with all the ruses we have employed to distract ourselves from our own vulnerability? When the fundamental impotency that has been loitering unnoticed all along at the peripheries of our self-confidence calmly steps forward to introduce itself? How should we act? Should we just carry on hoping that nobody will notice we are now only keeping up appearances? That is a lonely fate. Is it the only available option? To put on more clothes to hide one's shame? Can we conceive that life's worth living only if we can prove we have chosen the frameworks in which our activities happen? That we have been doing something instead of nothing? Most humans on Earth are barred access to such basics of choice. Like teenagers, they live in situations not of their own making, which they can do little to change but which could be otherwise; it is a pitiful testament to where our political and social practices as a species stand. But the fact that so many are starved for basics does not mean that the notion of freedom constituted by an unquestioned belief in doing something is therefore the summum bonum of human life. Is nothing worth doing unless it can allow us to sing back, "We did this; it wouldn't have happened without us"? Would we simply do nothing if there was ultimately nothing that could be done to change a certain outcome? Might we kill ourselves? It's a serious question. But while I respect the decision to perform the act, I do not propound it as a valid response to the situation in which there is nothing that can be done. (And I say this as someone who grew up in a family pervasively haunted by its violence.) There is still something—something that is neither the denial, nor the distraction, nor the dissimulation so often found in those who can do nothing other than demand: *Do something!* There is doing nothing. It is what you do when you finally admit that nothing can be done.

But I still could not rid myself of the suspicion that I was simply avoiding the elephant in the room: that I am mentally unwell and should do something to get better. For all my grim bravado, perhaps I, too, was unable to face up to the truth: that if doing nothing is in part an illness, it is also a truth about reality that cannot be erased until reality itself changes. Not just the reality of myself. Not just the reality of the middle-ground relations of human activity (the social, the communal, the ethical, and the political). Not even the reality of the environment and the global reach of the climate crisis. But the reality of the cosmos itself. In other words, there is no cure. And so I gave up. Nobody was coming to help. Taking counsel from the adage that misery loves company, I slumped down on the sofa and flicked through the offerings on some pretentious artsy streaming service. I was looking for something suitably depressing to match my mood. And I was successful. The Danish film director Lars von Trier turned up. A nobody I don't particularly like. So I started watching his 2011 film, *Melancholia*. Even by my standards, it counted as a real downer.

Lars von Trier's oeuvre comprises a sequence of films that is seasoned to an uncompromising degree. You can squirm into baroque contortions in your seat as much as you want, but nothing dissuades him from his course—and certainly not such decadent irrelevance as your precious comfort. Like a pit bull with a baby's arm, he does not relent. If anything, evidence of delicate sensibilities inspires him merely to tighten his grip further on the difficult, incendiary, and sometimes repellent material to which he is drawn—topics including sadomasochism and unconscionable grief in *Antichrist* (2009), intolerance in *Dogville* (2003), slavery in *Manderlay* (2005), and serial killing in *The House That Jack Built* (2018). And the list continues. There is an almost filthy, obscene quality to the whole endeavor. And this is only exacerbated by the parade of well-heeled stars (such as Nicole Kidman, Danny Glover, Catherine Deneuve, Lauren Bacall, and Uma Thurman) who have been prepared to work with him, even though (rumor has it) that's not always so nice. If you lay such luxury ingredients as the bodies of these performers atop such rancid narrative fare, things can really start to stink. And they do.

If this were not enough, it turns out to be short-lived to boot. His films quickly seem less an outrage than just tiring. It's not that they're no good. They are impressive, incontrovertibly so, and have been showered with awards and accolades. They are especially captivating regarding their formal innovation and wide-ranging stylistic palette. There is, for example, the signature handheld camera, low-budget, documentary style that von Trier and fellow Danish director Thomas Vinterberg first espoused in the 1990s in their famous Dogme 95 manifesto. And there are also forays into other modes, such as the abstract, schematic staging one might find in Brechtian theater: In *Dogville* and *Manderlay*, for example, the whole action takes place on a bare sound stage with the walls of the various buildings simply denoted by chalk lines on the floor. *Dancer in the Dark* (2000), staring Björk—who has made much in public since of the difficulties of working with the director—intersperses the no-nonsense Dogme 95 look with its veritable antithesis; breaking many of the so-called Vows of Chastity of the Dogme 95 manifesto, the film's musical sequences employ nondiegetic music and high-product color enhancement and make unambiguous reference to the standard genre type of the classic Hollywood musical.

Yet such impressive stylistic qualities contrast unflatteringly with the leaden insistence of the films' content. As a corpus of work, it is monotonously consumed with proving the validity of its grim vision. This is best summarized in a famous line from the very film I ended up being unable to stop watching, *Melancholia*. Spoken by the character Justine, in an extraordinary, career-changing performance by Kirsten Dunst, it is a blunt blanket condemnation: "Life on Earth is evil." It is enough to make one groan out loud. And oddly it reminds me of the European realist and naturalist novelists of the later nineteenth century, such as Émile Zola, whom I confess to finding similarly heavy going. Things easily devolve into virtuoso dramatizations of what might otherwise have been just sociological or existential platitude. In film after film after film, we are made witness to von Trier's characteristic maneuver of brutally stripping his characters of their accepted and acceptable social personae. Behind every type—the good neighbor, the political activist, the loving husband, and so on—the same evidence of moral bankruptcy and of an ethical void at the center of the human is unmasked. The expressionistic shock I suspect von Trier intends his audience to experience easily fades into more quotidian sensations of mild dyspepsia. I feel titillated, as by some Grand Guignol, rather than genuinely provoked to confront the shoddy reality of my ethical, moral, and political credentials. The point, after all, is somewhat low-hanging fruit. No, humans are not always very nice; I did get that memo, Lars, thank you!

Sometimes, I feel watching von Trier is a kind of hell; at other times, I find his work to be like the bad teenager I sketched earlier, or just embarrassingly like myself: shameless performances in which the director gets to pleasure his ego by means of uncompromising negative pronouncements—accompanied en route, I might add, by some pretty outrageous acting out.

Von Trier is therefore far from my aspirations toward doing nothing. Rather than helping me work out what I might do when there is nothing that can be done, he keeps himself busy torturing me with endless portrayals of situations in which there is absolutely nothing that can be done. That is, nothing at all. And that's not my point. Even when a situation is impervious to change, in most instances it still has space within it to move around in. What we do when we are moving around within it is what I call doing nothing. And what I've been trying to work out in my life is what is the best thing to do, and what is the best way to do it.

It is therefore odd that I found a solace for my dilemmas in von Trier's *Melancholia*, for in many ways, it would seem to be the magnum opus of his hubris. A rogue planet, eponymously named, is hurtling toward Earth. At first it seems that the swerve of its parabola will keep us from harm. As one character puts it: "Melancholia is going to pass right in front of us—and it's going to be the most beautiful sight ever." But as the film continues it becomes increasing clear that the planet is on a collision course and so there is nothing that can be done. The arrival of Melancholia is therefore far from beautiful. It is not something with which we can have enough space that contemplation and relaxed wonderment occur. Quite the contrary. We are to be brutally molested. The planet's arrival in the sleepy neighborhood of the irrelevant suburb of the C-list galaxy in which we reside will turn out to be sublime. Terrifyingly so.

Dwarfed into utter irrelevance by the total moral indifference of the universe, human life on Earth and Earth itself are to be iPad swiped out of existence. It is as if a quintessential modernist theatrical outrage is to be taken to the level of cosmological principle. We are to be made subject to a theater of such absolute cruelty that not only will the fourth wall come tumbling down, but everything sitting safe in the theater will be annihilated too. The arrogance of our human belief that we can get things done will finally be forced to confront its own true reflection in the cold black mirror of empty space. And then, irrefutably, we will know that nothing gets the job done properly like the meaninglessness of the universe. With that thought as our envoi, life on Earth will cease.

If *Melancholia* were only this, it would constitute either von Trier's most petulant revenge on whatever residual optimism we harbor or a kind of kitschy existential blockbuster. Think of *The Day After Tomorrow*, the 2004 film starring Jake Gyllenhaal in which a series of storms instigates a new ice age; now think of it again, but with no following day and also no tomorrow. The genius of *Melancholia* therefore lies in the uncanny counterpoint that von Trier sets up: Before the almost ridiculous epic backdrop, he makes a tiny ensemble of characters perform a terse interpersonal drama as circumscribed and integrated as anything in Jane Austen.

At the center of this chamber piece is a highly troubled woman, Justine (played, as mentioned, by Kirsten Dunst). In the first part of the film, we see her at her wedding celebrations, which are taking place amid the annoyingly tasteful grandeur of the house of her sister Claire (played by von Trier regular Charlotte Gainsbourg) and her incredibly wealthy but stingy husband, the absolute wanker John (flawlessly rendered by Kiefer Sutherland). An appalling lineup of work colleagues and execrable family members has gathered for the occasion, and it is one of von Trier's most impressive large-ensemble set pieces. Pretty much everyone is a scumbag. Von Trier lovingly crafts the swarm of damning details by which each of them has managed to avoid confronting what steaming turds they are as human beings. It is a virtuoso comedy that makes you want to slit your wrists, and Justine is lost in its midst in her tragedy.

Desperately hard, she is trying to go through with it all. As she says to Claire, "I smile and I smile and I smile." But it's not working. Claire merely spits back, "You're lying to all of us." And there is extraordinary cruelty to this retort. Because as Justine later says to the study in indulgent resentment that constitutes her mother (played with reptilian cruelty by an icy Charlotte Rampling): "I'm scared." Even though everyone knows she has a history of extreme and debilitating depression and mental illness, no one gives a shit. Nobody wants to know about melancholia—not even the sentimental idiot Michael (played by Alexander Skarsgård), whom she's just married. Claire gives not a fig about truth. Her complaint is simply the selfishness of someone who expects everyone to perform the smile of social convention with enough conviction that it eventually becomes what they believe. And she wants people to do so not because she thinks it's good for them, but merely so that she herself can then believe that everything is in place in the world and that she is therefore safe from harm. Rest assured, Melancholia will sort her out.

For now, however, Justine's acting skills are not up to the task. She is painfully aware of the artifice of her adult self— that it had to be rehearsed and learned—and that she now can't hold on to the role she's trying to perform or remember her lines. And so, at a certain point, to avoid being crushed to death by the demands of everyone else, she snaps and, in a sequence of exquisite terrorist maneuvers, trashes the whole wedding celebration and the married life she was just about to embark on. As her now crumpled husband leaves carrying his forlorn-looking suitcase, he says that it didn't have to be this way. But Justine is now cold with clarity: "But Michael, what did you expect?" He walks away. She watches him go. Her face is blank. She knows. There was nothing that could be done.

Between the first and second parts of the film, Melancholia metaphorically crashes into Justine offstage. At the beginning of the film's second part, she arrives once more at the house of her sister and brother-in-law, but she is now deep in a clinical depression of alarming magnitude. She looks less like a beautiful, talented woman in her prime and more like my earlier description of teenagers: an enormous broken toy whose batteries have run out, or an animal cursed to be subject to some unjustly increased force of gravity. But as the topic of the planet Melancholia starts to pervade everyone's consciousness, making them all increasingly freaked, Justine, by contrast, starts to recover and, in her own strange way, flourish. It is as if she gains inadvertent sustenance from the fact that everyone will now have to know what it's like to be destroyed by melancholy.

Part two of *Melancholia* is a rare space made available in von Trier's work for the possibility of seeing what we can do when there is nothing that can be done. It is titled "Claire" (the first part was simply "Justine"), but it could just as easily have been called "Doing Nothing." For even though we know the game is up, no one is rushing to put us out of our misery. If von Trier had given us just part one—parading before us all his usual damning evidence of the contemptibility of humans— and then called in planet Melancholia to summarily execute, it would have been a teenage revenge fantasy. But the more compelling second part of the film quickly makes us forget the bratty impotence of such acting out.

We are made to linger instead in a suspended condition of lassitude. It is an interregnum, and Justine, its warden queen. She presides with regal detachment and quiet indifference over this time. Passing away is the bogus reign of human hubris, given on loan to an unbalanced and delusional species by the sheer carelessness of Nature and her éminence grise, Contingency. And coming over the horizon is the triumphal return of the Empress Universe, whose law is to be brought to us by her emissary, the planet Melancholia.

Like any great statesman, Justine expresses next to no glee that her antiworld worldview has ultimately been proven right. She inhabits instead, in a zone beyond revenge, a kind of cool but gentle aristocratic confidence. It is not what she does that is of import; she carries on doing pretty much what she has always done before. She has a bath, goes blackberry picking, ponders which piece of chocolate to eat, naps. It is rather how she does it. The emphasis has shifted to style as opposed to action, form as opposed to content. There is a lightness to her. She is like a screen on a window; the air can now blow through. And there is a complete lack of urgency and the gritted teeth of determination. As a result, self-expression recedes, as if her attunement to the truth about the cosmos has started to dissolve the defining features of her individuality. And she no longer seems to need to signal to others that "it's all OK" and "everything is going to be *fine*!" She is neither exactly on the side of life nor clearly relishing the prospect of being dead. Oddly disconnected to what is going on around her, she is nevertheless

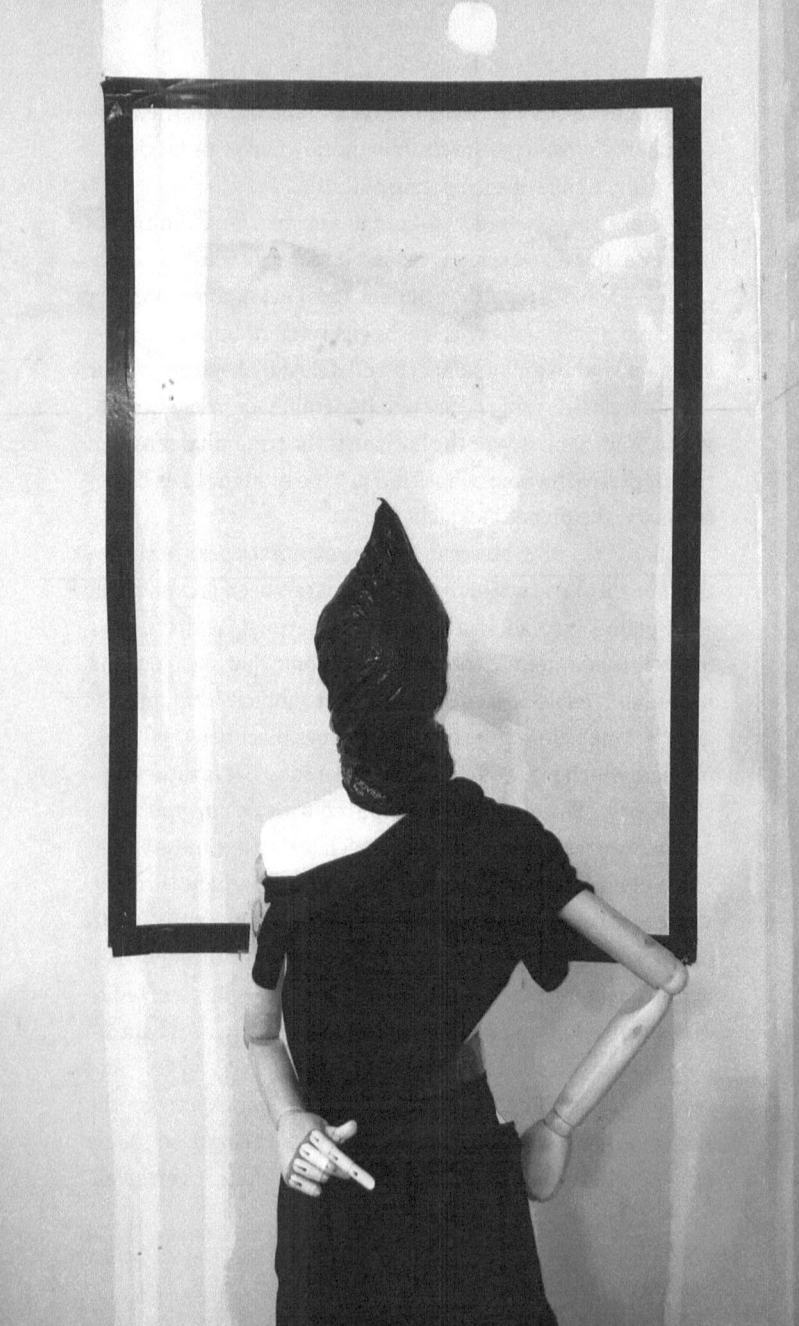

more capable of carrying on living in the face of what is happening than anyone else who remains. She has dignity. So much so, it is almost imperceptible. The guilty torments that had led to her terrorist destruction of her wedding and then brought her crashing to the ground of a clinical depression have gone. A mild contentment seems to glow just beneath the surface of her now otherwise bland affect. She seems happy, but without the added high-fructose corn syrup that constitutes joy. The strange experiment in manifestation and diversity constituted by lush and sexy Earth will end; we are to be brought back into alignment with the void ashtray aesthetic that constitutes the standard in this corner of the cosmos. For Justine, there is nothing to mourn.

In an extraordinary scene of trancelike strangeness in part two of *Melancholia*, Justine, seemingly alone, drifts out of the house at night. She moves as if subject to the profound influence of some secret master from another realm who has risen her from her bed and draws her toward the doing of his bidding. She glides across the wide stage of the lawn that silently extends with operatic grandeur away from the house, toward the river, and finally to the huge screen of the night sky, which rises at an impossible vertical at the horizon. She is dressed only in her nightshirt, a kind of waif bride. But it matters not. Issues of decorum have receded in the face of laws emanating from an entirely different register. And they are soon to be transcended. For having reached the edge of the lawn, Justine slips through the undergrowth and lays herself down on a rock. Naked.

Justine exposes herself. Quite literally. It is as if she were sunbathing, except that it is night. And not just any night, but a night in which the moon is now accompanied in the sky by the planet Melancholia. A night sky transformed by addition. Two instead of one. A prelude to the night of ultimate subtraction to come, in which Earth will be no more.

Lying naked on her rock, she looks up toward the source of this illumination as if she were looking into the eyes of a lover. And like someone on a beach in the sleepy hours of the afternoon, she touches herself lightly with a mildly indifferent and relaxed eroticism. But the light that showers down on her is eerie cold with tinges of blue, and the dreamy world of summer sun is eclipsed by a poetry shot through with qualities of sharp objectivity. Her body, as a result, looks less like it is porous, soaking up the nourishing rays, and more reflective. It is unnaturally bright and white, as if she has been drawn to laying herself out on this rock merely so that the planet Melancholia could come and see itself reflected off the surface of her torso. As if her role in this drama were ultimately to act as mirror.

Something of the almost fetishistic fascination of this scene comes from its inscrutability. We have inadvertently stumbled upon some sacred ritual intended for initiates only. It feels both thrilling and dangerous at the same time, as if the film has lured us into a trap in which we might be exposed as Peeping Toms. Which is precisely what threatens Claire, who, along with the camera and us, has been following her sister from a safe distance and now looks on, horrified and agog, from a hiding place in the bushes. The reflection of our predicament in Claire's draws us through the silver screen of the film's artifice into some fundamental and indisputable reality residing within.

Dramatized in this tableau is the truth that constitutes the entire film's point of perspective; everything else finds its place in relationship to it. And yet, like Justine—who, like Bartleby as described earlier in this book, loses the instinct for explaining herself as the film proceeds—this truth remains a mystery. It does nothing to reach out toward us with the gift of clarification. It is the strange mixture of strikingly focused at the level of image and completely cloudy at the level of meaning. Like some cryptic tarot card, it must be read. It is an allegory constructed of ambiguities.

Justine is here a mirror. And when we become such and only reflect what stands before us, we ourselves are canceled out. Being such was one of the preconditions I articulated earlier for becoming a hero of the doing nothing world. And Justine, for sure, is prominently featured in its pantheon. But as I move toward my end, I want to linger for a moment to think about mirrors in a broader historical frame.

The elevation of mirrors into a certain prominence in our habits of discourse, figures of speech, and turns of phrase was one of the ways through which the West entered its modern state, roughly around the beginning of the fifteenth century. And so now, today—as the climate crisis inches inevitably to irreversible, and human life from the emergency room to the hospice; as the networks of global capital proliferate, thicken, and tighten their grip, like muscles building up for a fatal heart attack; as wars sprout luxuriantly in expectation of natural resources dwindling further, and populations swell beyond sustainability; as we realize that, on so many levels, the game is up and, regarding fundamentals, there is close to nothing now that can be done; as history enters at last (surely) into what can only be the final drawn-out end of modernity (postmodernity, hypermodernity, liquid modernity, supermodernity, or whatever other euphemism takes your fancy), or maybe even as it enters into what might simply be the final drawn-out end per se—I am moved to think about mirrors again. To reflect on mirrors at the epoch's end—or, more specifically, on what we have let our mirrors reflect. To wonder what might have been different if we had turned them to face other things. Whether we might have found ourselves less hemmed in and claustrophobic, richer in spaces in which to move, and therefore able to practice different gestures and more expansive movements. Indeed, to wonder whether life might have been more danced than worked at. Less a time for getting stuff done and more a state of grace. Good enough in and of itself. Being rather than doing. A doing nothing, perhaps.

As the West crawled its way out of the black death and other traumas of the later Middle Ages—as general conditions improved and it started to become possible to view positive changes in one's life as resulting from modern entrepreneurial savvy rather than the vagaries of Dame Fortuna—it became increasingly common for the arts to start mirroring the world of human practices as precisely as possible. Perspective developed in painting, sculpture sought to re-create the appearance of the strict anatomical proportions of the human figure, an approachable and recognizable speaking voice in poetry and prose became audible, and in vocal music a more directly expressive relationship between music and text established itself as an ideal. And this all made sense. For when things are going well, we are happier to capture reflections of ourselves than when things are dispiriting. The presence of mimesis is a certain indicator of our well-being.

But as is made clear by the psychological fallout from our addictive relationship to social media positing—where we have learned too well to pull life-affirming facial expressions as proof we're having a great time—mimesis can just as easily be the handmaiden of denial and a prosthesis to compensate for where our lives lack. It is not just a contemporary problem. The photoshopping of our representations of ourselves long predates the emergence of the technological means for doing so. If the arrival of the early modern period in the West was accompanied by us picking up mirrors to feast on how fascinating we had become to ourselves—a habit retroactively christened *humanism*—there were other things that became difficult to look at and hard to know how to represent. The universe and where Earth was placed within it was one of them.

Medieval life may have often been extraordinarily harsh. But beyond its terrestrial difficulties, the distance offered comfort. It was still possible to believe that Earth was located at the center of an easily pictured, geometrically and mathematically constructed cosmos. The planets were ordered around us and, as they followed their various steady orbits, were thought to create cosmic consonances, the famous harmony of the spheres. However dissonant the immediacy of life may have been, we ultimately belonged to beautiful music.

Our solace came from centrifugal aspirations, spiraling outward to a larger, more reliable order. And this in part explains the medieval tendency toward allegory rather than mimesis. Music, image, and word were conduits to reaffirmations of a known universal plan. It was therefore fine that a medieval image of a human looks (to our modern eye, at least) more like a schematic cartoon than a successful representation of a living part of terrestrial reality. Because for the medieval mindset, a human was not solely such a thing; it was also part of the expression of the order of the universe. To represent it predominantly in terms of the specific appearances of individuals would therefore be to reduce it to something less than it was rather than make it more. To rob it of its dignity. From this perspective, the practices of Renaissance and baroque portrait artists therefore constitute a kind of myopia that enforces specificity at the cost of the broader picture, an inflation of individuals at the expense of cosmological truth. It is not unlike the way in which the individuals in *Melancholia* sustain inflated opinions of themselves so as not to hear the message coming at them from the universe. And to this degree, *Melancholia* is a kind of neo-medieval morality play in which those who prioritize their own belongings—their individuality, children, possessions, specific desires, worldly goods, status, wealth, property, and all the rest—are condemned to execution by the very cosmological truth that the hubris of their greed attempts to circumnavigate.

The fact that medieval cosmological comforts were based on a faulty understanding of the realities of outer space is to a degree moot; fictions are, after all, productive. And so even though they were scientifically in the wrong, their epistemological disadvantage made available to them a certain confidence. In terms of the universe, they still knew where they were; the universal meaning, relevance, and significance of their lives were still within their grasp. They were not yet lost. But then we went back and checked our numbers, started staring through our telescopes, and realized we were very wrong indeed. As a result, cosmologically speaking, we completely lost out. And more than four hundred years later, even with all the wealth of scientific understanding we have subsequently accrued, the brutality of this fact remains. We are nowhere. You would be hard pushed to be anywhere less central and more irrelevant in the humanly known universe than the cosmic backwater where the planetary crumb called Earth spins on its axis. The fact that scientific statistics show there simply must be a wealth of other life out there has in my opinion nothing to do with how we live. Thus, as an expression of affective reality, Justine's words in *Melancholia* are a pretty good summary of what constitutes our modern condition: "Life is only on Earth. We are alone." What we gained with modernity was the dreadful possibility that the human condition was one of ontological abandonment. We no longer belonged. And so we have, to all extents and purposes, been in exile ever since. To mask the embarrassment of this fact from ourselves, we have overcompensated by doubling down on who we are, the choices we have made, and all the stuff we've been getting done.

So what? Apart from the odd flat-earth lunatic in Texas, or an Arthur Schopenhauer here, or a Martin Heidegger there, few seem that bothered. On a day-to-day level, nor am I. It is just not news. Every now and again, I hear someone lightly caution— a mother to a child, perhaps—that it's best not to think about it too much; "drive you mad it will." But even then, there seems to be relatively little evidence of underlying tensions seething to force their way into consciousness. Such things are communicated at the same rhetorical pitch as any other "never mind" piece of advice. And I find this extraordinary when I think about

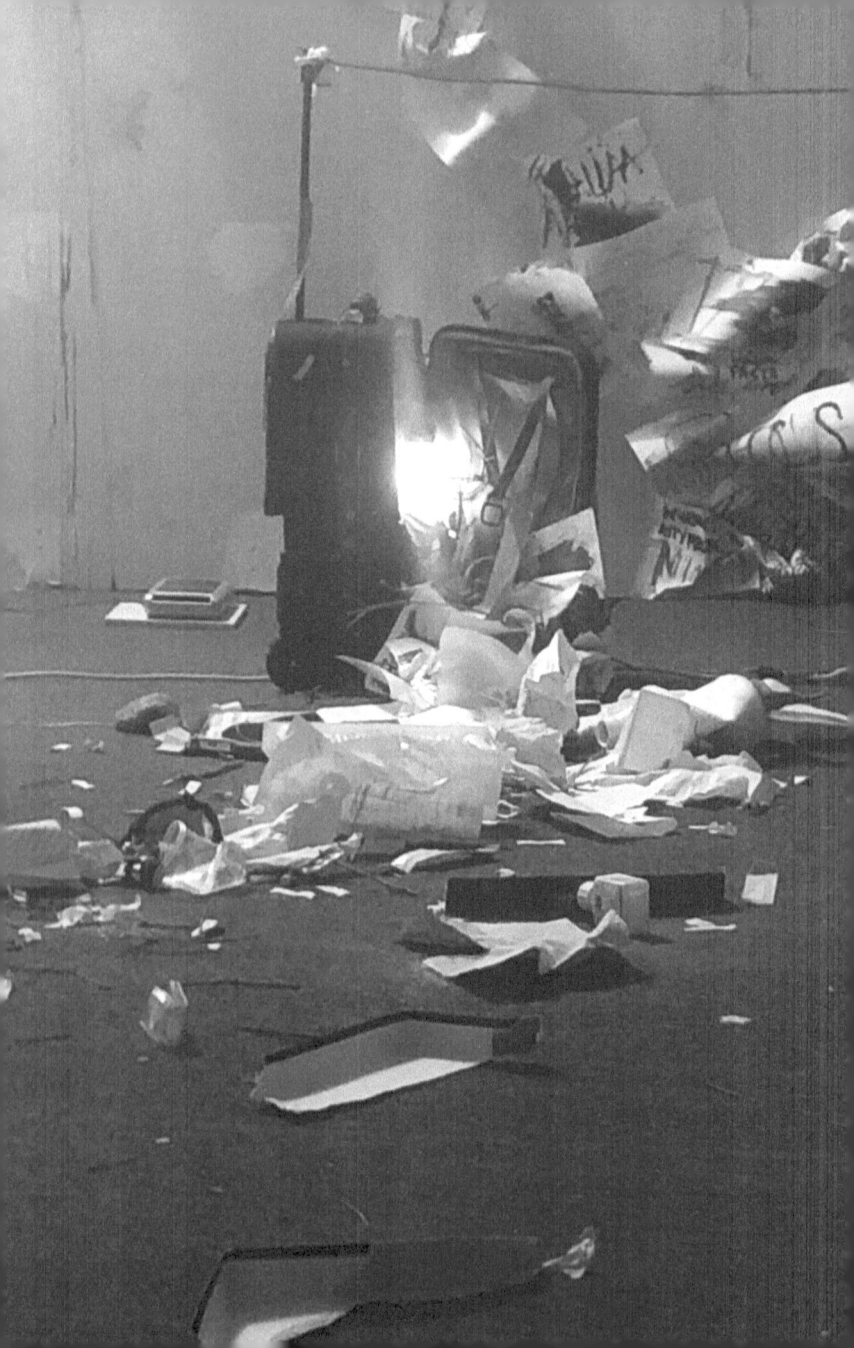

it. Humans were robbed of the ground on which to authorize the meaning of their existence in the universe. This is a big deal! Yet on the rare occasions when I hear anyone talk about it, their frustrations register little more than those attendant on catching a cold and not being able to attend a dinner party. "It's such a shame."

Faced with this, I feel the temptation to get blustery and pompous, to start hectoring about the increasing existential poverty of the human imagination, the myopic inanity of our cultural aspirations, and so on and so forth. But it's a little too easy, and probably to be avoided. What bowls me over is how staggering are the intuitive competencies of the human powers of adaptation. How relentlessly and belligerently it finds the means of making the vaguely habitable from the insupportable. This does not inspire me with optimism. But it does, irrefutably, consume me with admiration at its immediate level of practical, technical achievement.

My mother's life is torn apart by mental illness, and yet she staggers through a self-imposed, rickety, homespun program of recalibrating herself to an alarmingly reduced orbit, and, more than a quarter of a century later, she's still here managing a pretty good impression every now and again of getting on with things in a chipper fashion. Or there's the human species, overcrowding a minuscule planet and finding itself vulnerable to a highly infectious and lethal flu variant. Its only hope is to impose restrictive practices at a global level of coordination that is unknown in its history and, from a theoretical point of view, seemingly inconceivable in terms of the structural inability of nations and their various legal protocols to find their place in relationship to one another. And yet COVID-19 comes, it finds its position, and we continue to live in awkward dialogue with its developing presence. But live we do. If that is not so well, it is still far in advance of what the early, more apocalyptic prognoses had foreseen. And then there is the fact that the human animal was bestowed by nature with unprecedented brain power. As a result, it finds itself with thinking capacity left over from covering its basic needs, and it employs that excess to build telescopes that then destroy the illusions that had made its life seem livable. Four hundred years later, it has worn that trauma down so that it registers barely more than a suburban ripple in the teacup of quotidian life. This is a species that is consumed, from the local to the global, by insomniac practices of adaptation to the endless destruction of its lifeworlds. It is really doing something. The question is, at what cost?

Much of this book has been a personal testament to what I have thought about in my situation—a situation in which I have lived within certain structural conditions, particularly psychological ones, about which there has been nothing that could be done. But if things got a little dark, it was never the intention to suggest that one should simply lie down and die. The fact that I am inclined to find the act of not doing much to be perfectly acceptable—that I can easily be found staring out the window, or lying on the floor gawping at the ceiling, or taking the train to the end of the line for no other reason than to then take it back again—does not mean that I am averse to the idea that my thinking might lead to action. Nor does this action spurn the habit of adaptation that I have just been admiring in my species. Obviously not. For if doing nothing is what you do when there is nothing that can be done, then logically speaking one's whole existence is a kind of adaptation. We all must live within the nonnegotiables of birth, death, illness, and loss, within a cosmic condition from which the guarantors of meaning have departed. The issue is not whether one adapts; it is how one decides to do so. Doing nothing is simply a way of sustaining a certain attitude to adaptation: that faced with a situation whose fundamental coordinates cannot be changed, you adapt in a way that does as little as possible to obfuscate, belittle, dilute, write off, gaslight, censor, ignore, distract from, or sideline those nonnegotiable coordinates. Doing nothing is therefore sometimes adamance, even belligerence; it is con- stituted by a refusal to deny. But it is not, as a result, a kind of manning up to the heroics of truth. Or even, for that matter, an attempt to live life in quest of truth.

What's at stake here is less how we establish the truth than what to do when truth is something that *happens* to us—in those situations where we trip up over it unexpectedly. When truth becomes our fate. When a nervous breakdown confronts you with the underlying psychotic structure of your psyche, or when playing around with a telescope reveals the crushing fiction of your cosmology and the vertiginous eradication of the terra firma on which your constitutive notions of yourself had rested.

Sometimes we trip up so hard we have no other option than to stop what we're doing and try to take account. But our ap- titude for adaptation easily encourages us to make a dash for it. Sometimes this dash is a kind of desperate pragmatism— because the truth is too traumatic to bear. But at other times it is simply an attempt to escape the constitutive paradoxes of human fate. Because the very brains that allow us to stabilize our territories by means of adaptation have powers left over (and restless desires that encourage them) to keep thinking once the act of adaptation has been completed and there is no longer any need. We are the twitchy animal. As a result, we are constantly threatened with encountering the very truths that could destroy the territories from which we had been thinking. What allows us to make home also allows us to destroy it. We are all our own Pandoras, and the precarity of our existence is as much a result of what lies within as of what lies beyond. The homespun wisdom that counsels us not to think too much is thus, to all extents and purposes, a pragmatic philosophy wielded against nature and truth. And in our unnaturalness, we can be quite successful indeed—managing to live in a high-functioning state of denial of the very things that have disturbed. This is what I argued adults do to escape the truths revealed to them in the strange limbo years of their adolescence; they work hard to practice new lines and, through the mantra of their repetitions, blot out evidence that anything else could be done.

But what damage must be done to everyone else who must weigh down their lives to support such delusions? What about all those who cannot make the dash successfully to the safety of denial? Plenty don't. I haven't. What about them? Are they simply doomed to truth? What are they meant to do with what they've seen and what they now know?

In the early stages of modernity, we looked through a telescope and our cosmology fell apart. But we still have telescopes today and have continued to look through them. Indeed, we have developed them to extraordinary degrees of technological sophistication and have surrounded them with armies of specialists who are economically funded by sources emanating from the most powerful forces of governmental and economic control on the planet. If we lost our position of being at the center of the universe, then one of the ways we compensated was by making telescopes a point of focus. Around them we have attempted to reconstruct the sense of meaning that telescopes themselves had been responsible for robbing us of. There is a gnarled dialectical sophistication to this that—once more, in testament to human powers of adaptation—I cannot help but admire.

But how have we continued to look through these instruments? What kinds of desires have come to mediate the increasingly enhanced information they have allowed us to receive? How as moderns have we looked into the vast voids of space? Since the telescope figures prominently in both parts of the film, von Trier's *Melancholia* offers us two hypothetical answers. There is Justine's way, and there is the way of her brother-in-law, the execrable John.

John is a psychological study, in the classic von Trier vein, of a multimillionaire. Fundamentally tight when it comes to financial transactions with others—griping, for example, at having to pay for the cab fare from the station when Justine arrives amid her clinical depression—he is nevertheless extravagant in bestowing gifts on himself, and tetchy about anyone else messing with his stuff. He is a greedy bastard, and he has a fabulous telescope.

For John, his telescope in part is simply a means of indulging an amateur interest in astronomy. (If he wasn't so awful, someone might recommend him to Duke University Press to write a nice little book about it—*Stargazing*, perhaps—for its Practices series.) But his telescope is not only the means of him enjoying looking into outer space; it is also a means of him being able to enjoy looking at himself. It has been instrumentalized as part of the technology of his narcissism. It is a prop that allows him to perform a role not available in the rest of his life—where he is a nasty little nobody who has accrued wealth through poverty of moral imagination. With his telescope at his side, however, he can access a certain sober-minded wonderment, rather like one of those nice scientific experts that used to populate nature series on TV. ("Full of mystery is the vastness of the universe, and we humble ourselves before its inscrutability. But with the patience of science, through generations of accumulated investigation, we will one day find the answer to the questions of who we are and why we are here." This is the kind of schtick I imagine echoing in John's gold-lined trash-can head while he is feasting his eyes on the firmament.)

As a character in a film, John is verging on parody—which we can justify as realism to the extent that in real life people of his ilk are a sick joke. But contemplating his representation in the film allowed me to conceptualize a certain response to the existential trauma that instigated our modern world. Like a figure in an allegorical drama, John stands for those who are prepared publicly to admit that we no longer know where we are, but only because they have convinced themselves that we will eventually regain what we lost at some higher level through the patience of modern scientific research. His repeated alignment of himself throughout the film with what he calls "the experts" is therefore not belief in science at all; science is just a ruse for an elaborate fait accompli. The proof of this comes when he ultimately realizes that Melancholia is not simply going to pass Earth by; it's going to destroy it. At that point, the thin performative crust of his rational certitude collapses into the stinking refuse pit of his craven solipsism. It is a classic von Trier maneuver. John steals the pills that Claire, his wife, has secretly stashed away in preparation—should John's predictions prove wrong and they all need to commit suicide—and takes them all himself, leaving his "lovely" wife and his "beloved" little boy to face annihilation without anesthetic. Once he realizes there is nothing that can be done—because the universe turns out to be completely indifferent to the self-serving notions he harbors about it—he can only depart, lie down and die. He is so on the side of life that he becomes incapable of doing anything at all with the time of life that remains. Maybe, as I suggested earlier, he would have been a better human if he had practiced a diversity of alternative distances and spatial positions in relationship to the significant points of reference in his existence rather than just holding on for dear life to the crap he decided was his. At any rate, so much for those who claim to be doing something.

As Bruno Latour, the French philosopher, waggishly remarked, we have never been modern. John's relationship to modern science in von Trier's *Melancholia* is proof of this. Rather than taking on board the distinct possibility revealed to us at the onset of modernity—that we are a mistake in a universe devoid of meaning—he opts instead for a compromise and recoups medieval cosmological certainties in the form of deferral. (The certainties we once held were wrong, but certainties there are. Although we lost our home, we will eventually make it back to where we truly belong.) What we came to call modernity was really just an attempt to create a heroics of the human, of dealing with fear by means of self-aggrandizement. For what could be more impressive than a micrological human somehow managing to answer the riddle of an inconceivably vast universe.

As we stagger toward the epoch's end, it seems clear how disastrous such projects have been. But as I stagger toward the end of this book, it is worth speculating how it might have been otherwise. And maybe wondering if there is still time left for that to take root. So I turn finally to the heroine of my book. To Justine.

Justine and John are at opposite ends of the moral and philosophical spectrum. But they are linked by the fact that they are both drawn to things astronomical. John's relationship, via his fancy telescope, is ultimately one of compensation; the telescope is a prosthesis for everything in himself that limps. Justine's, however, is stranger, more feral and intuitive, as if she were, in some neo-medieval way, in tune with the universe. Her relationship fuels her rather than compensates. Early in the film, when she arrives ridiculously late for her own wedding reception, she looks up into the sky as she is about to enter the house and points to some almost invisible, tiny star. She asks what it is. In his own patronizing fashion, John is impressed that she can perceive it at all. It will, of course, transpire to be Melancholia. Soon everyone will be able to see it all too well.

As the disaster of her wedding celebration escalates toward its grisly conclusion, Justine periodically takes respite from the guests by going outside alone to look through the telescope as it sits, quiet as a bomb, in the grounds of her sister's house. Like

John, she is fascinated. But her interest is fueled by very different objectives. For John, the telescope allows warm validations to be served with a cooling sauce of sober scientific blab. For Justine, it is existential sashimi: raw evidence that no such validations exist. It is by feasting on this pure philosophical protein that she ultimately acquires the nutrition necessary to get her back on her feet from her clinical depression and to start helping her sister and heartbreakingly lovely nephew, Leo, to prepare for their end in the wake of the passing of the era of John. She is cured by opting for truth rather than attempting to salvage stability. It is because she accepts that there is now nothing that can be done that she becomes the only person competent to do anything at all with the time that remains. She is liberated from the endless difficulties of her own life, and from the exhaustion produced by her repeated inability to do something to resolve them. She is doing nothing.

The tragedy of Lars von Trier's *Melancholia* is not, then, that Earth is destroyed and with it a record of the history of human achievement; it is that the model of an alternative way of being never got the chance to flourish. It is not that the past will be lost, but that an alternative future will never sprout. We have suffered so much to do something—and made so many others suffer so that we could hold on to our suffering privileges—but rarely have we indulged in the pleasures of doing nothing instead. So what might those pleasures have been?

Over the time spent writing *Doing Nothing*, I came to wonder if they might have been as follows: not the pleasures attendant on the liberation *of* ourselves, but rather the pleasures attendant on allowing for the liberation *from* us of everything else. A liberation of existence from the human. And maybe

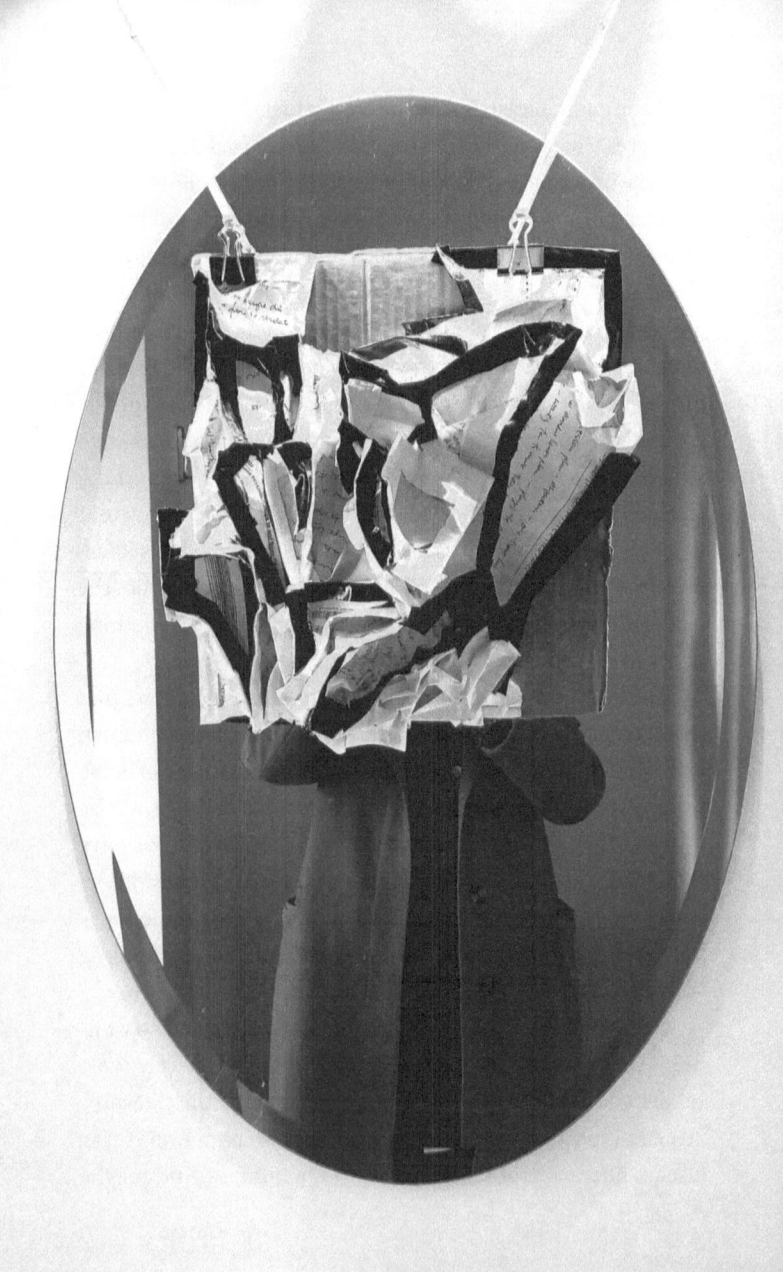

a liberation of the human from the human, too. This is what is radical about Justine lying on her rock, exposing herself to Melancholia, and giving herself up to the fact that there is nothing that can be done. At this moment, she turns herself into a mirror. But unlike the mimetic mirrors of humanism and the ensuing modern epochs—which helped us to adapt to the horrors of a meaningless universe by diverting our attention to celebrating the wonders of ourselves—this is a mirror turned out into space. Justine becomes the means of reflecting only that which is *not* her. She cancels herself out so that the universe can then look at itself.

Her act of what I would call existential decorum should not be thought of as selflessness, or being humble, or any other such worn-out, cod, feel-good term. Once we start talking like that, we are right back with the moral narcissism that has underwritten our acts of denial—a moral narcissism that, in our contemporary moment, comes to a head in the plague of virtuosic virtue signaling that has morbidly infected discourse. Rather, such existential decorum would be a kind of Epicureanism, a hedonism to be practiced like a discipline. Because if we could liberate nonhuman existence from its condition of having to help us to deny, then that existence would also be liberated from having to appear through the grimace of our forced positive feelings. Justine therefore exemplifies a new kind of practice for humans on the planet, which is to offer the nonhuman the opportunity to smile for its own reasons. And so even though I have made you loiter with sometimes rather unrelenting fare, my aim has been likewise. To show through doing nothing how to learn at last to smile.

Preface

1 Hodgkinson, *How to Be Idle*, xi.

2 Northrup, *Do Less*.

3 Lutz, *Aimlessness*, 30–31, 39, 52, 67, 107, 143, 149.

4 Jonat, *Do Less*.

5 Muradov, *On Doing Nothing*, cover.

6 Mecking, *Niksen*.

7 Odell, *How to Do Nothing*, xi, xxii (emphasis original).

Part 1. About Me

1 William Shakespeare, *King Lear*, act 1, scene 1.

2 Melville, "Bartleby," 112, 113, 116, 117, 118, 122, 126, 140.

BIBLIOGRAPHY

Hodgkinson, Tom. *How to Be Idle.* London: Hamish Hamilton, 2004.

Jonat, Rachel. *Do Less: A Minimalist Guide to a Simplified, Organized, and Happy Life.* New York: Simon and Schuster, 2014.

Lutz, Tom. *Aimlessness.* New York: Columbia University Press, 2021.

Mecking, Olga. *Niksen: Embracing the Dutch Art of Doing Nothing.* London: Piatkus Books, 2020.

Melville, Herman. "Bartleby, the Scrivener: A Story of Wall Street." In *Billy Budd and Other Tales.* New York: New American Library, 1961.

Muradov, Roman. *On Doing Nothing: Finding Inspiration in Idleness.* San Francisco: Chronicle, 2018.

Northrup, Kate. *Do Less: A Revolutionary Approach to Time and Energy Management for Busy Moms.* New York: Hay House, 2019.

Odell, Jenny. *How to Do Nothing: Resisting the Attention Economy.* New York: Melville House, 2019.

von Trier, Lars, dir. *Melancholia*. Hvidovre, Denmark: Zentropa, 2011.